Front Row, Section D
by John Hitchcock

Produced, edited, designed, typesetting, and layout by Billy Ingram

Title ID: 4968556   ISBN-13: 978-1500956196

I wrote this book with these people in mind:

Bobby, who used to watch wrestling with me.

Morrie, who never gave wrestling a second thought.

Sparky, who took me to my first match at the Coliseum.

Wiley who gave me a kidney so I could keep going
to wrestling.

And my mother Amy. If she knew what I was doing
all those years she would have had a fit.

This book is dedicated to the above and all the fine folks
who attended Professional Wrestling matches with me.

Table of Contents

Introduction

Professional Wrestling was always a part of my life.

In North Carolina, South Carolina, and Virginia you really could not escape Jim Crockett Promotions, a family owned Professional Wrestling Organization under the National Wrestling Alliance, in business for over fifty years. And Greensboro was the place were all the big name wrestlers flocked to.

Why?

At one time the largest building between the Omni in Atlanta and the Cap Center in Washington, DC was the Greensboro Coliseum which could seat around 9000 people; later expanding to 15,500 then topping off ten years later at 23,500 seats. Charlotte could only accommodate 8000, Raleigh a little less than that. For that reason alone Greensboro became the hottest wrestling venue in the Mid-Atlantic.

It was all about money, imagine that.

That and the fan base was scorching hot for years and years. The television market opened up in the early sixties and, before anyone could notice, interest in the sport grew like weeds in summer. Everyone I knew went to wrestling or talked about wrestling from grade school on for the rest of their lives. Yeah, it was a part of my culture, it was that ingrained.

Thanksgiving was especially a big deal. We would get up, watch the parades on TV, have a wonderful turkey dinner around lunchtime, watch the Detroit Lions get their ass kicked, take a nap to sleep off the meal, then go to the coliseum for a night of Mid-Atlantic Championship Wrestling. That was just how things were done back in the sixties, seventies, eighties, well into the nineties.

We saw the greatest wrestlers of all time here in Greensboro for about five to six bucks a ticket. Names like Flair, Funk, Arn, Tully, Brody, Hansen, Ole and Gene, Blackjack, Steamboat, The Rock and Roll Express, The Midnight Express, Ladd, Cornette, Dillon, Bolos, Weaver and Becker, Rip and Swede, Odell, Dykes, The Infernos, Stevens, Super Destroyer, Wahoo, Valentine, and Race. You get the idea. It was a Golden Age that the now-old farts like me talk endlessly about.

Wrestling is still around. It comes to Greensboro like the circus, once a year. But we all know that stuff sucks, we'd seen the best the sport had to offer for years. The WWE never has been able to measure up to Jim Crockett Promotions. Period.

I hope you enjoy this book. And if you don't like Professional Wrestling, please do not talk to me.

About this book's cover: During the period that photo was taken Dusty Rhodes was wrestling under a mask as the Midnight Rider. His intro music contained the lyrics, "You can't tell the book by looking at the cover" so...

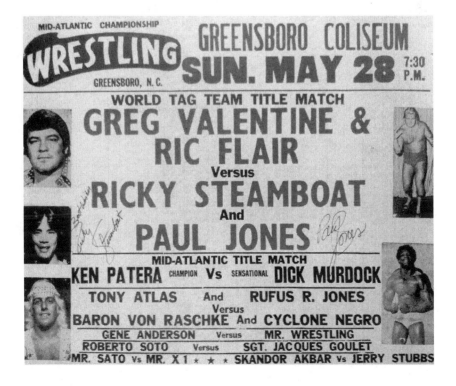

Anything with a Ring and Chairs

I started watching wrestling at age 10, in the mid-sixties. I remember watching a tag team match with the flying Scott Brothers vs a couple of losers, it was all a comedy. I turned around to my older brother Sparky and said, "This is better than the circus!" From that point on I was a fan.

I think most wrestling fans started that way but most moved on to other interests. I continued to watch whenever I could. My brother Sparky worked at the Greensboro Coliseum as an usher and on wrestling nights was responsible for bringing the grapplers drinks and oranges before the matches.

One of those moments you never forget: Sparky said, "Yeah, its all fake. The wrestlers hangout and talk over the matches. Rip Hawk, Swede Hanson, and Johnny Weaver (pictured), they're always playing cards. And one weird thing; do not talk to Brute Bernard, he just sits in a corner drooling on himself. He is crazy."

Now that's important stuff to know. Wrestling is a show and it allows psychopaths to earn a living. Only in America...

The seeds were planted; I became a wrestling fanatic. Any show, any promotion, I would watch anything with a ring and chairs.

Sparky took me to my first house show in 1966. The main event was for the Eastern Heavyweight Title; the champion the Missouri Mauler versus Danny Miller.

I always liked the bad guys even at this stage. They do all the work and nobody ever cheers for them and it seemed to me the Heels always said the funniest things!

I got to see the underworld that night. Such stars as Luther Linsdey, Joe Turco, Rip Hawk, Suede Hanson, Klondike Bill, and George "Two Ton" Harris. The Coliseum only held 9,000 then, with no upper deck. As I walked into the arena, Sparky said, "Remember, the entertaining part is half in the ring and half in the stands. These people all look like they fell off a turnip truck." And he was right. This one old guy was yelling, "Head-butt him, LUFFER!" as he continually dropped his bottle of wine.

I went home crushed as Miller took the title from the Mauler with his finisher the Chicken Wing Cross Face. I went home dying for more and I guess I turned more people into fans than just about anyone. Every kid who moved into the neighborhood would end up watching wrestling with me, maybe that is why so many families moved out.

And then a miracle happened. The family down the street got Cablevision!

In a few weeks I got cable! That opened the door to more wrestling! Think about watching a Saturday full of wrestling, WWWF, Georgia, 3 hours of Mid-Atlantic, Florida, and a strange show shot in a tent called All Star Wrestling.

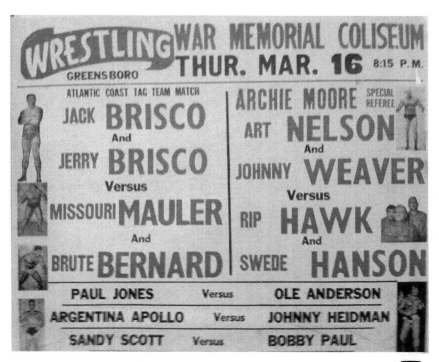

There Should Be Statues

And those statues of wrestling stars should be in front of the Greensboro Coliseum. After all, they built that enormous barn for wrestling, not the ACC tourney.

Tag Teams

Before we get too far into this I want to shine a spotlight on a few early wrestling legends that generally get overlooked. Tag Teams were the main event in the Mid-Atlantic all during the sixties and into the early seventies. That's when I first started watching wrestling as a kid. These guys made a huge impression on me for a lot of reasons. Mostly, tag teams were always stocked with odd, goofy heels that were funny as hell. And some were menacingly scary guys too. Please note this was when I was ten to fifteen years old.

The Bolos

These guys should be mentioned first, they had a very serious edge to them. The Bolos did not clown around and seek laughs during their matches. They kicked the shit out of everybody and told you ahead of time what they were going to do. They had a monster run against Johnny Weaver & George Becker and Weaver & Haystacks Calhoun. They wrestled everywhere else as The Assassins but as the Bolos here. Back in the fifties there was a masked guy called The Great Bolo so Crockett promoted them that way. They had a drop-dead great heel interview style. After awhile the Bolos changed their names to The Great Bolo and Bolo, I could never really tell them apart. There was an angle that is burned into my head, a huge feud brewing with Johnny Weaver and Haystacks Calhoun.

Haystacks wrestled as a hillbilly with a beard and bib overalls, he weighed about 550 pounds. He also carried with him a metal horseshoe on a chain that he used when things got tough. Yeah, I know what you're thinking, he beat people up with a foreign object and the refs didn't do anything about it? Now you know why I always cheered for the heels. And before I forget, Haystacks never washed his gear so he smelled like an elephant's asshole in July.

A televised match had the Bolos vs two "'young lion" job guys, best two out of three falls. This match started with one of the Bolos grabbing up his opponent, dragging him into his corner and beating the snot out of the poor guy. After tagging in a few times they then pinned him.

After the commercial break, The Great Bolo is cutting a heel promo to end all heel promos. He told the audience that beating was just a taste of what Weaver and Calhoun were going to get in Greensboro, watch the next fall and see for yourself. The tag team rules back then were if you took the fall, you had to start the next fall.

This young wrestler proceeded to get another ass kicking for about ten minutes. It was nasty, the Bolos just crushed him again! Then after pinning him, (his partner never even got in the ring), The Bolos cut another brutal interview saying Weaver and Haystacks were toast. I have never seen anything like that before on TV. It was two bad ass guys proving just how serious they were in glorious black and white. We didn't have a color set yet.

George Becker and Johnny Weaver

These two without a doubt were the Baby Face tag team of all time but if you see a photo of them you would never believe it. Weaver was the main baby face forever in this territory and, I suppose, was a good looking guy in his youth. Becker looked seventy when he was thirty so there was absolutely zero sex appeal with this team that I could see. The way I heard the story is that there was a tag team back in the fifties called the Becker Brothers and George was part of that. Odd, but the other Becker, Bobby was really named Becker, he died in the ring. He had cancer but continued to wrestle until he took a body slam and never got back up. That was when Weaver came along and tagged with the established George. I would bet Becker and Weaver wrestled together for at least 20 years and about 360 dates a year. They would be the good guy champions until a monster heel team would come along and feud with them... and there were a ton of heels to deal with.

Back to Weaver and Haystacks. When they got together, George Becker was tossed aside like an old shoe. This did not go over well with Becker so he started up his own outlaw promotion going against Crockett. Hard to believe but this group did get on local television, I watched it religiously. It was a small time show filmed in a high school gym with a bunch of second-stringers at best. Becker did the color commentary and I cannot remember the play-by-play guy at all.

This show only lasted a month or so, a huge mess but I loved it! It had an atmosphere that anything could happen and it felt dangerous. The one thing I remember clearly is the time Becker snapped during a taping and went after a heel to set up the big feud. You could tell that the old guy had popped his cork and was really going to beat this guy's ass, match or no match. The promotion was dying, losing money, and Becker just went nuts. That was the thing about television back in the sixties. You didn't need a lot of capital to get your show on. Television stations sold the ad time but would get the show for free. Poor old George Becker, that was the last time I ever saw him in a ring.

The Flying Scott Brothers

George and Sandy Scott were the first tag team I ever watched on television and they really did fly all over the ring doing the "gasp," Flying Drop Kick move. Yes boys and girls, that was a finishing hold back in the day. Note, I am trying to sound cool and up to date and sadly I am not. And they were really brothers! George Scott later became an excellent booker for Jim Crockett Promotions. He was the guy who booked Wahoo Mc Daniel, The Super Destroyer and Johnny Valentine. Sandy worked behind the scenes just about everywhere. I met him once at the box office selling tickets for Smokey Mountain Wrestling. I did like the Scotts when I was young and innocent buying everything as fact the promotion said. That changed very quickly with the next team.

Rip Hawk and Swede Hanson

These two guys were really the first truly cool heels I can remember. There was a wry sense of humor in all the interviews Rip Hawk did. Rip did all the talking and Big Swede could do all the heavy lifting. Rip used the pile driver as his finishing hold and Swede utilized the swinging neck breaker to set that move up. In an interview Rip said that Johnny Weaver looked like a taxicab with both doors open. Later on Playboy Gary Hart managed this duo. When I was a kid I loved Gary Hart. He once got his head kicked in at a special event-boxing match against Weaver. Hart juiced all over the place and was left lying. My old pal Harry swears I began to tear up during this match. I think he was right. But Hart coined the phrase, "One day the Big Swede will lay a Big Harry Knuck up side your head!" Big Harry

WRESTLING SALEM SAT. 13
CIVIC CENTER APRIL
PRICES: RINGSIDE $3.00 - RESERVED $2.50 - GENERAL ADMISSION $2.00 CHILDREN 12 AND UNDER $1.00 **8:30 P.M.**
TICKETS ON SALE AT: CIVIC CENTER, & USUAL LOCATIONS

TEXAS DEATH MATCH
GEORGE BECKER AND JOHNNY WEAVER
Versus
RIP HAWK AND SWEDE HANSON

SPECIAL EVENT!
MR. J. C. DYKES Versus NELSON ROYAL
(MANAGER OF INFERNOS)

TAG TEAM MATCH
THE INFERNOS VERSUS ABE JACOBS & LUTHER LINDSEY

JIM GRABMIRE Versus **PAUL JONES** ★ **BOB NANDOR** Versus **LEE HENNING**

Knuck soon became a catch phrase around my neighborhood. Rip and Swede wrestled in this territory forever and with Weaver and Becker 1200 times a year, at last count, for at least 10 years. Later Swede had a heart attack and a wrestler was brought in for his replacement. A brash young cocky 300-pound fireball named Ric Flair.

Aldo Bogni and Bronko Lubich

The big deal about this team was their manager Homer O'Dell, he was Mister Heat in the Mid-Atlantic territory. O'Dell used a cane as a foreign object and that drove every fan crazy. But what would you expect? This was the first time anyone had seen a manager, or a gimmick to cheat with. O'Dell also was a really solid, arrogant interview, that drove his team to titles. Aldo and Bronko used a knuckles to the temple finisher that, I think, was called The Crusher. It looked really painful too, ask my little brother. I used to slap that one on him all the time! That and the Japanese belly hold could make anyone scream in pain. Try it on your kids, loads of fun for the whole family! Fan scuttlebutt was that O'Dell was a wild man in real life and a legend in Charlotte for throwing naked pool parties. Racy stuff to hear when you were eleven.

The Infernos

This team was masked and wore all red gear so that both guys looked the same except one of them had a built up shoe, a wedge on the right side of the boot. Whenever the referee got turned around Inferno would tap his foot a few times on the mat and kick his opponent to win the match. The opponent who took the boot shot sold it like a bazooka blast and would take the pin. Everybody believed it was a loaded boot but the Infernos manager J.C. Dykes said sometimes the poor guys foot would fall asleep and that was how he got the blood going again. I always looked up to a

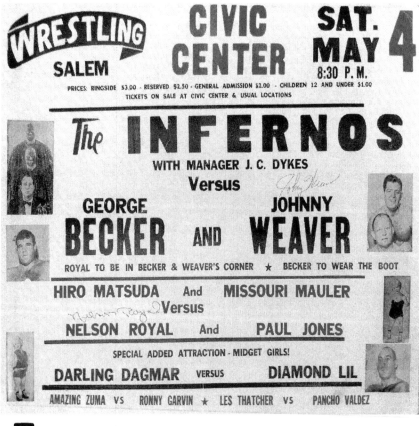

guy who is handicapped and overcomes this to feed his family.

Dykes carried with him a metal canteen just in case his men got thirsty. What a guy! Sometimes fans detected him hitting his opponents with it but hey, guys got to do what a guys got to do. The Infernos also used the old foreign object in the mask head butt trick. This gimmick was so funny, why didn't it knock both guys out? Fans theorized that the mask was padded or he was so used to it because he did it so many times. Or maybe his head is harder. Stupid fans, you got to love them.

Once Weaver took that famous boot from the Inferno and rattled it on an interview to prove it was loaded. Weaver and, I think, Haystacks sought revenge at the next big show. This bothered me because poor Inferno needed two boots to wrestle—and Weaver did steal his property. Why didn't he call a cop?

Always remember rasslin fans, reality and wrestling have nothing in common except gravity.

The Royal Kangaroos

Lord Jonathan Boyd and his cousin Norman Fredrick Charles the Third were one of the most entertaining tag teams of all time. I loved these two guys, talented and athletic. They used a finisher where they would beat an opponent until he was sitting in the ring, that's when Charles would get a running start and cut a summersault with all the pressure falling around the guy's neck.

Boyd and Charles did incredible condescending

heel interviews that to this day stand out as brilliant and funny. They talked with an Australian accent and flat out talked down to every announcer that ever interviewed them. Boyd had this elitist patter, felt it was beneath him to talk to an American. And Boyd would then set up Charles for a funny remark. Their timing was incredible.

The Crockett promotion was setting up a feud with Thunderbolt Patterson coming in the feud with the Royal Kangaroos. So Boyd started talking trash, why would royal blood ever want to deal this commoner Patterson. Boyd would grind out the words, "Thu- Der-Bolt Padder-Son" in his interviews with total contempt. Then Charles would throw in his line that would inevitably bring down the house.

Charles once said excitedly, "You know what cousin, Thunderbolt Patterson is so dumb he thinks a pig pen is something you write with!" And with that they both started laughing and walked off the set.

You had to laugh with them. So you figure that Thunderbolt was coming in and kick the shit out of them, right? Well, the money offer must not have been good enough to bring Thunderbolt in at this time for the feud, or he was really hot at that time in Atlanta, because he was a no-show. It was strange to have such a super build up then nothing came of it. What did Lord Jonathan do? He cut a brutal interview telling everyone Bolt was a coward and that they hunted him down and crushed him. There was Boyd holding a T-Bolt straw hat torn to pieces in his hand telling every one to look at what it left of Thu-Der-Bolt Padder-son.

The Royal Kangaroos then had their big feud with Johnny Weaver and Art Nelson for the Brass Knuckles Championship Trophy. Nelson was a muscle-bound fireplug with little charisma. I was there for that match, the Royal Kangaroos beat the hell out of Weaver, and Nelson turned heel and walked out on him. The heat was scorching, fans wanted to kill Nelson for leaving. "The Weave" to the wolves. Both teams spilled buckets of blood in this match, The Royal Kangaroos celebrated in the middle of the ring their Brass Knucks Trophy.

After this big run here in the Mid–Atlantic, The Royal Kangaroos kind of disappeared from sight. Years later, I spotted Boyd on a Memphis Tape, he was very heavy and working as a jobber. That kind of broke my heart. Boyd and Charles deserved a much better fate.

The Kentuckians

Big Boy Brown and Grizzly Smith. Sorry, the only thing I remember about this tag team was that they were good guys and carried a powder horn with them to hit wrestlers with. That and they wore blue jeans and plaid work shirts to the ring.

This was the classic backwoods gimmick that I hated. Because I'm from the South and surprise, I have most of my teeth. I do not chew tobacco or have a still in my basement. I have two degrees and I do not rassle gators or carry a pig with me to work. Now and then I do want to be a Double Knot Spy but that is about it.

The Southern stereotype irritates me, we ain't that way. If you want to think Southern, think Mayberry. Those characters were shown to be warm and friendly people. I can live with that. But this stereotype dominated wrestling for decades. For example, The Moon Dogs, Haystacks Calhoun, Hillbilly Jim, Man Mountain Mike, Mighty Wilber, Little John and the despised Uncle Elmer. How could any one from the South ever cheer any of those guys?

Nelson Royal and Tex McKenzie

Old time fans would be screaming if I didn't mention Tex and Cowboy Bob Ellis but they were before my time. Nelson Royal was a fixture in the Mid-Atlantic, I'll bet I saw a thousand of his matches over the years. These guys became the cowboy tag team with Nelson doing the wrestling and Tex talking in his homey drawl to draw the fans in. Tex was the first wrestler I remember being fairly clumsy in the ring, he would trip on the ropes and stuff like that. Tex did have a great down home shucks type interview style and was about six four, very tall for a wrestler. He also was the first that ever took off his cowboy boot and kicked the shit out of the bad guys with it.

Paul Jones replaced McKenzie after a few years. Number One Paul Jones was another guy who wrestled here forever. Nelson owned a western leather and clothing store outside of Charlotte. The Crockett's were always filming promos at his place. He sadly became a little nuts at the end of the eighties. I met him once back in the late nineties, he said he would love to talk more but had to leave right away to work a house show in

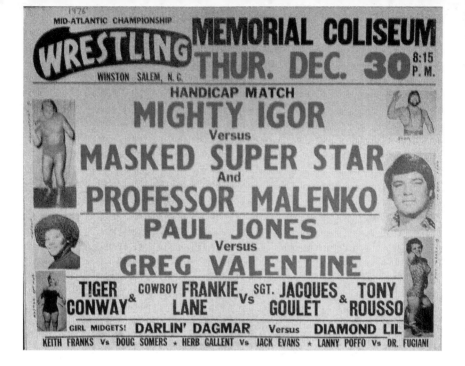

Raleigh for Crockett who had been out of business for about ten years, so I worried about Nelson Royal.

Bill Bowman and Joe Turner

These two were the first tag that I ever witnessed that attempted to be "gay" in the ring. These two big men wore pink tights, pink boots and pink ribbons in their hair. Of course they hugged before every match. They were low middle of the card at best and fans truly hated them. I don't remember them lasting in this role very long. And they were really tough guys before this attention-grabbing role. In 1970, nobody was marching for these guys' rights.

The Anderson Brothers

First there was Lars and Gene Anderson. Lars did all the talking with a bulldog face on a cinderblock head. Gene would do all the wrestling and stand behind Lars using this odd tick he had, twitching his neck in a very odd fashion. This was a real life mannerism he had and it worked like a charm, made him look mean and unbalanced.

Lars quit the team and Ole Anderson was his replacement. To long time fans Ole and Gene became wrestling royalty when The Minnesota Wrecking Crew was born. When you mention the great talkers in wrestling history Ole Anderson is flat out the best of his generation, and maybe the best ever at talking fans into the arenas.

The Andersons wrestling style was total no nonsense. They would cut the ring in half, keep you in their corner, and then work on one body part until their opponent would submit. Their signature move was holding an opponent's arm behind his body then slam him on it over and over. Afterward, Gene would hold the guy's arm out for Ole to jump off the top rope for the submission. The opponent would be yelling in pain, this worked so well the Andersons were feared.

Ole once used the phrase, "A three legged chair can not stand!" and they proved it night after night for years in the Crockett territory. (Three-legged

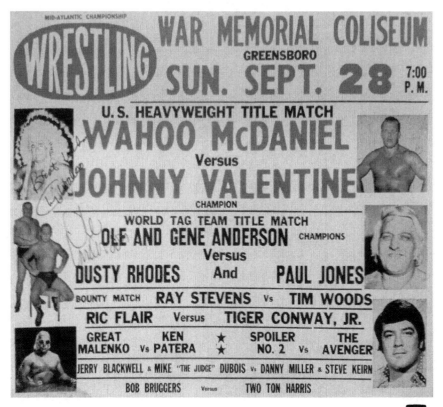

chair… I guess Ole never heard of a stool?) Fans would go crazy as Ole or Gene lured their foes into the corner where they would rarely ever let them out again. I mean it, the heat was incredible because all the fans saw week after week the same moves so they knew what was coming and they didn't want their favorites to get hurt.

Simple, direct repetition psychology executed flawlessly by brilliant performers is what great wrestling was all about. Once the Andersons were in a TV match against Wahoo McDaniel and Paul Jones. This match was pushed very hard as the Andersons' last chance at the World Tag Title. Wahoo and Jones had their way the whole time tossing Ole and Gene around the ring. The finish was a true classic that everyone over fifty remembers. Gene, outside the ring, was yelling for Ole, "Do It! Do It!"

Ole grabbed Wahoo to propel him head first into Gene's head, thereby sacrificing him for the Title win. Gene fell to the floor unconscious while Ole rolled up Wahoo for the pin. Interviews later saw Ole screaming at the television audience that the titles mean so much to them that they would kill themselves to keep them.

Everyone believed every word, The Anderson Brothers were tough as nails.

MID-ATLANTIC CHAMPIONSHIP
WRESTLING
LYNCHBURG ARMORY
LYNCHBURG, VA.
FRI. APR. 21
8:15 P. M.
RICKY STEAMBOAT
And
TONY ATLAS
Versus
CYCLONE NEGRO
And
GENE ANDERSON
MR. WRESTLING Versus JAN NELSON
CHARLIE FULTON Versus DON KERNODLE
BRYON ST. JOHN Versus TONY ROUSSO

All Star Wrestling

All I know about wrestling is best summed up by a crazy, violent TV wrestling show that came on television in the late sixties at 12:00 on Saturday morning. I swear this program looked as if it was shot inside of a tent. This alone caused me to drop everything in order to schedule my day around it. Anything could happen on this show, everything that was great grappling was squeezed into that insane hour.

The spectacle started out with a lot of splashed colors, over which was written All Star Wrestling accompanied by some weird background music that sounded like someone trying to kill himself playing bongo drums. I laugh about that intro to this day.

My favorite angle was when they introduced the sadistic heel, Killer Buddy Austin. I had never seen this bruiser before, come to think of it, none of these characters looked familiar.

Austin was a tall, tan, white haired veteran that seemed as if he despised being there, the prototype of what all Heels strived to be. Hated.

On one episode there was this squatty green jobber in the ring that angered Killer Buddy who did the gentlemanly thing and piledrove his ass on to the concrete floor. Superb action and beautiful execution—only one problem.

The piledriver was an outlawed move in this tent so Killer Buddy was to be suspended. Oh the shame! The pinhead fans in attendance, all 37, enthusiastically agreed

Souvenir PROGRAM

OLYMPIC AUDITORIUM
FRI. SEPT. 2, 1966

25c

World Heavyweight Wrestling Championship

BUDDY (KILLER) AUSTIN
Champion - St. Louis

A MRS. CAL EATON SPORTS PRESENTATION
JULES STRONGBOW, Matchmaker

since the squatty jobber was flailing around the ring in pain like a trout out of water.

The announcers were convinced that the "young lion" would be crippled for life by this move. (Note, if they call you a "young lion" you will never win a match, same is true if you are called a "wily veteran"). Next week, as special guest, there was Squatty with a neck brace on, sitting alongside the announcers.

They showed the terrible attack again, the violent carnage that seemingly would put poor Squatty out of work. Turned out Squatty had a family to feed—who would have thought it, this guy was making a living in wrestling!

Well, old Squatty starts yelling (I swear this is true), "I will get you Killer Buddy Austin!" sounding as if he read it off a cue card. Suddenly, from behind the curtain, Killer Buddy charges out to annihilate this guy. The announcers, in classic hurried terms, yelled, "IT's KILLER BUDDY AUSTIN! IT's KILLER BUDDY AUSTIN!"

Squatty, still sitting at the table, was attempting to turn around but the neck brace made this impossible, he resembled a stuffed sausage squirming around as he screamed, "WHERE?"

In an instant Killer Buddy ran up behind him and snapped Squatty's injured neck like he was opening a beer. Oh, the humanity of it all! I laughed my ass off and I'm still looking for footage of it to this day.

So the very next week the announcers asked Killer Buddy to come out and explain this outrage. Austin stood by, visibly pissed off, as they replayed the tape of all his evil deeds from the past two episodes. "What do you say for yourself, Killer Buddy?"

"That's trick photography," he cried. "I never did that!" The show came back from commercial with a standby match featuring "young lion" Indian Jay Whitecloud or was it White Wolf?

As the newcomer stepped into the ring Killer Buddy went on the attack, ramming the young lion's head into the ring post and piledriving him to the hard studio floor. As they were going off the air the referee held up Billy Whitewhatever's head exposing a major league gash screaming blood into the camera. With a childlike glee the announcer yelled, "Look at this ladies and gentlemen, this is not fake! This is real! Our wrestlers are real!"

This show taught me all about the classic heel build up, the sad underdog challenger angle, and what wrestling was really—a morality play.

Hi, I worked with Buddy Austin, fought with Austin in and out of the ring. Had dinner with his wife and kids. Buddy Austin was my best friend. There has never been any wrestler who did not know he had been in the ring with Buddy for about 4 or 5 days after the match. Or if he found himself in a bar with Buddy he never forgot it!

As Lou Thez said he was and will always be the world champ. (Lou won the WWA World championship and it would be Lou's last from Buddy in October of 1966 and lost it to Mark Lewin in two weeks).

Buddy had a heart as big as anybody in the world, but he was the last wrestler you wanted to piss off. My question is, do you have any of Buddy's matches at all? I know that all the KTLA Los Angeles Wrestling was burned in the early 1970s.

Also when you watched what he did in that tent you laughed - what you don't know is he was not playing a game! To be in the ring with Buddy Killer Austin it was as REAL as anything gets! To Vince his dad would have told him, "There is no hall of fame without KILLER AUSTIN."

- Alan Colker

I was the president of the Buddy Austin Fan Club in Los Angeles back in 1967, 1968. I had the opportunity to personally meet Austin, he was a great guy in and out of the ring. It was such a tragic event when both his children died in a pool accident, I believe at their Tarzana house. That was basically the end for him and his lovely wife Carmelita. They moved to Hawaii after that and his career ended there. Thanks for the memories!

- Shftmar

WRESTLING

LYNCHBURG ARMORY

LYNCHBURG, VA.

FRI. APR. 10

8:15 P.M.

6 MAN TAG TEAM MATCH

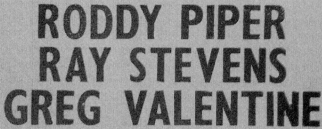

RODDY PIPER
RAY STEVENS
GREG VALENTINE

Versus

SUPERSTAR
PAUL JONES
JOHNNY WEAVER

JIMMY SNUKA Versus CY JERNIGAN

GENE LEWIS Versus **BRUNO SAMARTINO, JR.**

KURT VON HESS Versus **ABE JACOBS**

MID-ATLANTIC CHAMPIONSHIP
WRESTLING
LYNCHBURG ARMORY
LYNCHBURG, VA.
SAT. MAY 5
8:15 P.M.

13 MAN
BATTLE
ROYAL

$6,000.00 TO THE WINNER
5 BIG MATCHES IN ALL
BARON VON RASCHKE
DINO BRAVO ★ PEDRO MORALES
STEVE KEIRN ★ MOOSE MOROWSKI
GARY YOUNG ★ PAUL ORNDORFF
JOHN STUDD ★ SKIP YOUNG
SWEDE HANSON ★ BRUTE BERNARD
FRANK MONTE ★ DAVID PATTERSON

Southern Poster - Atlanta, Ga. (404) 873-8194

27

How Cablevision Made Me A Genius

I was very fortunate to have cable TV in the mid-sixties, Greensboro was one of the first cities in the nation to get wired. It took me about 20 seconds to realize I now possessed a tremendous power.

The Mid-Atlantic Wrestling Show would come on three times a day. At 4:00 from Raleigh, at 5:00 from Winston Salem, and a repeat show at 11:00 out of Winston Salem.

Doesn't exactly sound like the keys to infinite wisdom, does it? Oh man, how wrong you are grasshopper!

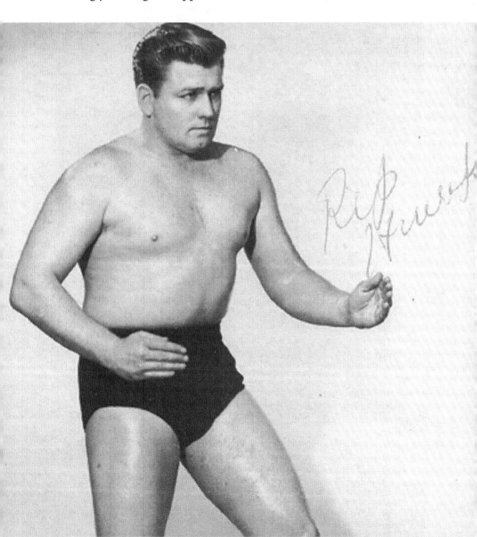

Starved for good booking ideas the fine folks who produced the series, Crockett Promotions, would repeat angles—the same Heels with different faces. What a hoot! And it set up my personal road to ultimate wrestling power.

One day Crockett ran an angle with Playboy Gary Hart and Rip Hawk where Hart claimed that no one in wrestling can last ten minutes with the great Ripper and put up one thousand dollars in cash to prove it. Out comes Jerry Brisco of the famous Brisco Brothers to accept the challenge.

The match lasted about seven minutes and what do you know, Jammin' Jerry pins the fifty year old Hawk. Well, into the ring struts the Playboy waving ten one hundred dollar bills to state he's a man of his word and will pay his debt to weak link Brisco. Hart starts to count out the money, one bill at a time, with the television crowd cheering along with each bill. One, Two, Three, and at Ten he misses Brisco's hand.

Brisco bends over to pick up the last bill and was vulnerable to Hawks finisher, the piledriver. Taking full advantage, Hawk drops Brisco on his head while Gary Hart scoops up the cash, kissing the loot with great gusto.

Brilliant. But at 5:00pm they did the exact same angle!

Only the chump this time was long time face Johnny Weaver . I had a group of friends stop by and I told them, "He's going to drop the last bill, watch and then Weaver is going to be in the perfect position to be piledriven by Rip Hawk." Lo and behold, it happened just that way.

Man what a pop at the Hitchcock household! All my pals started yelling, "How did you know that?" So I gave them the scoop and we all realized Johnny Weaver must be the world's dumbest wrestler for falling for what happened to Brisco just an hour earlier. Or maybe Crockett didn't know about Cablevision.

So from then on we created the Johnny Weaver Dumbass Award for every time something stupid like that happened.

Why Harley Race Rules The World

John with Harley Race

Let me make one thing very clear, I hated the faces during this period. Nothing has changed that much in my way of thinking. The Heels did all the work and got none of the glory. And one more observation: the faces would get pissed off at any disrespect from the audience, especially anyone cheering against them.

I really had it in for Magnum TA, the pretty boy face of all time—he hated me. I am not making that up. Maggie May never liked being reminded that he sucked. Imagine that.

On the Front Row with a few enlightened friends I made a sign for Magnum. This was a few years before the Front Row Section D days to come but I would never miss a chance to light up Magnum. So when Mister TA came out I held up my poster reading: FAGNUM PU. Not my best work but it did the trick.

Magnum shot me his classic look of death. It took very little to get this guy riled. Out to the ring comes, to everyone's surprise, Harley Race. Shit! Race was a legend; many time NWA champ and nobody's punching bag.

I started going off on Magnum, getting into his head that Harley was going to kill him and show the world he wasn't half the wrestler that Race was. Sounds pretty trite but a man has to do what a man has to do for entertainment.

Race entered the ring and, ladies and gentlemen, we had the real deal going down in

Greensboro that night! I ain't kidding. Race beat Magnum like one of Michael Vick's puppies. Gave the guy no quarter whatsoever in the ring, the ass kicking of my dreams.

Race looked at the sign I was still holding up and heaved old Fagnum down to the canvas, laid him out right in front of me. Race gave him a stiff punch in the back then scooped him up and threw him out of the ring on to the concrete.

I swear the guy bounced off the floor twice. Brutal. At that point Race screamed, "READ THAT SIGN, BOY!" so I stood up and almost put the damn thing right on top of Magnum.

That did nothing for Magnum's temper. So good old Tommy Young does the old classic count out DQ finish as we all chant, "HARLEY! HARLEY!"

As Race was leaving the ring, I got in Magnum's shit, "Hey Magnum! Are you gonna let that old man kick your ass like that? I thought Greensboro was your town. Are you gonna let him get away with that?"

He took the bait. Magnum grabbed the microphone and yelled, "HEY RACE! NOBODY DOES THAT TO ME IN MY TOWN! COME BACK TO THE RING!" I just about lost it. Harley stopped, turned around, walked calmly back to the ring, looked right at me, smirked, then said—and I quote—"I already kicked your ass once boy, I guess I have to do it again."

We started cheering for Magnum's execution, "HARLEY! HARLEY!"

You know the point in every match where the heel attacks the face as he goes through the ropes? Magnum did that to Race. Race refused to sell and grabbed Magnum by his hair and heaved him over the top rope like a Frisbee, literally spinning sideways. Magnum busted his ass and, as he attempted to get up, Race chopped him in half with some brutal punches before slamming him again full force on the concrete floor, with no give, then spit on him and walked away.

As Magnum staggered to the back room I continued yelling at him that this was his town and he should ask Race back one more time. As Harley walked to the back he yelled back to Dusty Rhodes, "I JUST KICKED YOUR BOY'S ASS AND IF YOU DON'T LIKE IT, DRAG YOUR ASS OUT TO THE RING AND I'll KICK YOUR FAT ASS, TOO!"

Eat shit Rhodes! My hero!

The next day I got a phone call from a friend who was working third shift at 7-Eleven. He asked if I went to rassling last night. Oh yeah! And Magnum got his head handed to him by Harley Race.

"Oh, did you make any signs?" "Yeah, yeah." "Well, Magnum came into my store last night and I asked him how the matches went. He kind of blew me off; he had a hot blond with him and was buying a sixpack. I mentioned that I had a friend that always goes to the matches and makes signs. Magnum loses it, "YOU TELL THAT GODDAMN SON OF A BITCH THAT I WILL GET HIS ASS!" Then he hurled his beer to the floor and stormed out of the place with his chick whining, 'Magnum, I want some beer.'"

So there you have it. I found out later that it was Dusty Rhodes that brought Race over on short notice to job for Magnum so he would get a shot at the World Title. Problem was Race was too proud an athlete to lie down for his pal. Believe it or not, Magnum told Harley Race that they should settle it in the ring.

Same thing happened in Charlotte with the Masked Superstar Bill Edie. The Superstar had just come off a long tour in Japan teaming with Dick Murdock and was brought in to job for Magnum. It took about two minutes for that ass whipping to finish. The Masked Superstar then walked to the backroom and quit the promotion to head for New York.

Both Race and Edie would have no trouble with anyone from that time period, probably still could handle themselves to this day.

Wahoo McDaniel

Growing up in North Carolina, everyone knew "Wahoo Mac Danel." Most of his fans knew him with that pronunciation. At school, at work, at the park, it was "Wahoo Mac Danel."

I was at some of Wahoo's greatest matches. I was there to see him in the ring in Greensboro against Johnny Valentine. Folks who attended those matches still talk about them. Not out of some nostalgia but because no two men hit each other any harder than those two. You could hear the chops and hammers in the upper deck, believe me, but you had to be sitting in the first five or six rows to have sweat and blood splash on you to really comprehend the Legend of these two men.

Years later, I met Wahoo on at many independent shows, and I am proud to have given him a poster with him versus Johnny Valentine listed as the main event.

I had several from which he could chose. "I'll take Valentine. Everyone still talks about him," he said. Wahoo told me he framed that poster and put it in his den. Like most old-school wrestlers, he saved very little memorabilia. People talked to him about those days but the poster brought it all back.

I wish I would have bought more autographed photos from him. But I was way to intimidated to do it. And it was a sad sight to see him being passed by as kids got pictures from younger stars.

I was in Greensboro when he battled against Ric Flair, the next best thing to a match with Johnny Valentine. The biggest difference was Flair would sell for Wahoo. Hell, he had to.

The image of Flair selling the Big Chop off the ropes is something that I will remember forever. Flair, bloody and squirming like a freshly run over dog, that image is still fresh in my mind.

One night on the Front Row I watched Wahoo get hit so hard he collapsed ringside. Kim Duk must have gotten pissed at him and, as Wahoo was turning the ring corner, Duk hit him with as hard a blow as I could remember. Wahoo never saw it coming. That sound still haunts me.

I was there in Greensboro during the tag team days. Ricky Steamboat, Paul Jones, and Tim Woods could tell you stories. I was there when Wahoo turned heel with Tully Blanchard. People talk about heat. Brother, you don't know heat until you sit in Raleigh, or Charlotte, or Richmond, or Greensboro. The fans would believe.

People often ask me why I am a wrestling fan. Today it is a little hard to defend. The heroes of my youth are fading. That's why I'm honoring these men. It was real to so many folks who made a religion out of Mid-Atlantic Wrestling on Saturday nights.

And The Big Chief was the star.

Florida on Cable

In 1968 my family subscribed to Cablevision and my television world exploded from three stations locally to multiple broadcasters from around the country.

You cannot imagine the impact. For one thing you could finally see the picture clearly. This opened my world to Florida Championship Wrestling which I instantly recognized as the big time. That was saying something because I grew up in the bloody Mid-Atlantic and already knew the goods.

The first show I caught by total accident. A friend of mine was going nuts talking about the Great Malenko getting badly beaten and bleeding all over the place. Well, I had to see what that was all about. The local cable station had this wrestling block set up with two hours of FCW in a row on Saturdays so you could watch the last week's show and then see the new broadcast next hour.

I walked into Robert Cummings house and sure enough there is some Russian guy yelling at this huge wrestler. He was in a rage because he had lost his match. Suddenly the big goof snapped and beat the hell out of Malenko! I do not think I ever saw a guy bleed so much on TV. Well, anywhere for that matter. Nobody rushed in to help pull the big guy off. It was brutal. And the amazing thing was my friends thought it was the funniest thing they had ever seen.

From that moment on I was hooked on Florida grapps. I never missed a show. One day I even broke into a neighbors house to see the show. I was totally into it, the amazing bookings. It became my soap opera. There was always an amazing cast of talent that was carrying the story along.

My favorite from that moment on was Boris Malenko and it seemed he was the ultimate classic heel. Every thing revolved around this driven insane guy.

The big four of Florida were Gordon Solie the classic announcer that could make anything seem possible and believable. Solie was just amazing at getting over the faces and very carefully let you know that the Heels were the bad guys.

He was the constant that the whole show relied on to make sense of this sweaty mad world. And it was not easy but Solie did it with ease. The second was Eddie Graham the owner and booker. Quite frankly the man was brilliant and he could tell a story and could direct you from one action to the next flawlessly. This is a tough thing to do.

Graham would often appear as the proud father, the color commentator or the enraged observer. It all depended on what was needed to make the story clear. And I am sure he made money, after all that was the point.

Third was Malenko. As I said, he stirred the drink. And now I am going to cheat. Really the third are all the great Heels that followed Malenko too. Graham booked so you would hate the Heels so much you would cheer the faces no matter who they were. Face it, Jack Brisco was a tremendous wrestler but he was dull as paste on the microphone.

And fourth, the ring was amazing. The sound of the wrestlers falling had a metallic sound that made everything feel so devastating. The power that sound had coming over the TV, it sounded like they were killing each other taking a bump. No other ring had that ping.

That was my introduction to the world of Florida and I don't think wrestling was ever the same for me.

The Big Cat Ernie Ladd

Ernie Ladd, without a doubt, gave the funniest interviews week after week. Even now if I want to have a few laughs with my friends I'll slip into my Ernie Ladd impression, yelling at everybody in sight.

Ernie Ladd must have been inspired by a Tex Avery cartoon from the fifties about a big old loudmouthed bear wanting to hire a watchdog so he could get some sleep. Any little sound would wake him up and the bear would scream, "SHUT UP! QUIET! SHUT UP! WHAT IS WRONG WITH YOU! ARE YOU DEEF OR SOMETHING?" etc.

That was Ernie Ladd in a nutshell. And his post-match interviews were always the same rant. Here are my favorites combined into one for your entertainment.

"Yes, mister TV announcer! I am Ernie the Big Cat Ladd! I am six foot nine, three hundred pounds, and size 17 shoe! And I am tired of all these wrestlers walking around talking out the side of their necks! Staying, YAK, yak, yak. YIP, yip yip, I do this, I do that! You ain't doing nothing to the Big Cat Ernie Ladd! Do you smell whiskey Gordon Solie?"

"Aaaaahh, no Mister Ladd, I do not."

"It must be that drunken Indian Wahoo McDaniel! I hate Wahoo McDaniel! I hate him! He is nothing! Wahoo is nothing but a drug store Indian with a cigar stuck in his mouth! Nothing worse than a drunken Indian! He needs to be sent back to his reservation and I am just the man to do it! Shut Up! I am tired of it!"

"I am Ernie the Cat Ladd! I am six foot ten, three hundred and ten pounds, size 18 shoe! I here tell that there is a fat man walking around saying that he is the American Dream? He is nothing! American Nightmare is more like it! Dusty Rhodes! Dirty Roads is more like it! He ain't nothing to the Big Cat Ernie Ladd! Shut up Rhodes and tell the truth! You have been running from me for years! I chased you in Florida. I chased you out of Texas! You are nothing but a coward Dirty Roads!"

"I am Ernie The Big Cat Ladd! I am six foot eleven, three hundred and twenty pounds, size 19 shoe! I am a man to be feared and respected! I

was an All American in football at Grambling College and I have a Super bowl ring with the Kansas City Chiefs! And I am unbeatable in the squares circle! Isn't that right Gordon Solie?"

"Aaaahhh, that remains to be seen Mister Ladd."

"Shut Up! You don't know nothing about the big man, Ernie Ladd! Where is that puppy dog Buzz Sawyer? There should be a leash law in this town! Mad Dog Buzz Sawyer! He ain't nothing! I will beat him! I will destroy him!"

"Because, I am The Big Cat Ernie Ladd! I am seven feet tall, three hundred and thirty pounds and size 20 shoe! Rufus R Jones! Where he at? He ain't nothing to Ernie Ladd! I beat his cousin Burrhead to within an inch of his life! And the only reason I didn't kill him was because I like beatin' him!"

"That is the truth! I tell the truth! Rufus R Jones is an Uncle Tom and I hate Uncle Toms! The Freight train is no trouble for The Big Cat Ernie Ladd! If I beat up his family then maybe he will get some guts and face The Big Cat. I have no respect for Rufus! He step and fetch too much for me!"

Johnny Weaver

Johnny Weaver has always been there.

When I started watching TV he was on the very first show and I guess he always was. Weaver was tagging with George Becker and were feuding with Rip Hawk and Swede Hanson.

And I guess he always was.

Weaver was the top face for a long, long time in the Mid-Atlantic, he got the big title shot against Lou Thesz, Gene Kiniski and then Dory Funk, Jr. The matches always went the hour time limit to a draw with Weaver at the brink of victory, holding his own against the best and leaving with his pride in tact.

After a short while, I began to hate his baby face act. Humble, thoughtful and respectful of the promotion. Weaver became a sap in my eyes, it was not his fault. He just looked so bland in comparison to the Infernos or the Bolos.

Those guys seemed much more cool but Weaver had the tough job. He had to play the good guy and really never could attract the cheap heat Heels got with just a glance or a smart remark. I bet he wished he could have mouthed off to Skull Murphy or Brute Bernard or slapped the taste out of J. C. Dykes or Homer O'Dell's mouth. But he was the good guy. He was a clean slate to create heat off of. The guy you had to play against to create the story. And it wasn't an easy thing to do.

One night at the Greensboro Coliseum they announced that all the wrestlers would be out front signing autographs for the fans. This turned out to not be totally true. There was no table for the heels. I was hoping to get Brute Bernard to bite or drool on my program. Now, that would be a great collectable! But there was a table for the faces and a small group were signing for the fans.

Les Thatcher was there greeting fans, so was a really green black grappler called The Night Train, he was a large, strong looking guy but only lasted about a month then was gone. Art Nelson was on hand too.

And, of course, Johnny Weaver was there chatting up a flock of old ladies. Weaver was very patient with these folks, showing them all the scars he had on his head. "This one came from Homer O'Dell hitting me his cane." This went on and on.

When Weaver became an announcer I really could not stand him but he was a lot better than David "Homer" Crockett. One night Johnny Weaver called Barry Windom's flying clothesline finisher, "The Flying Thing Off The Ropes." I fell off the couch laughing.

Then one day I pissed Weaver off. It was a Starcade where half the action took place in Atlanta. We all got dressed up in really bad clashing suits and I brought a dozen pair of those red and blue 3-D glasses.

We were sitting about ten rows up in the orange seats in order to see the big screen above the ring. I told everyone to put on the glasses and, whenever a wrestler would bounce off the rope in front of us, we would sell it by jumping back into our seats. It was a real attention grabber that's for sure.

For fun so I yelled down at Johnny Weaver, "Hey Weave! Why don't you paint one of your ears red and the other one blue so I can get a real 3-D effect with your ears! Come on Weave!"

That did not go over very well with him. Weaver got up from his announcing table, threw down his headphones, and stalked off the set. Jim Ross was sitting beside him, he was pretty pissed too.

Hey, can't ya take a joke?

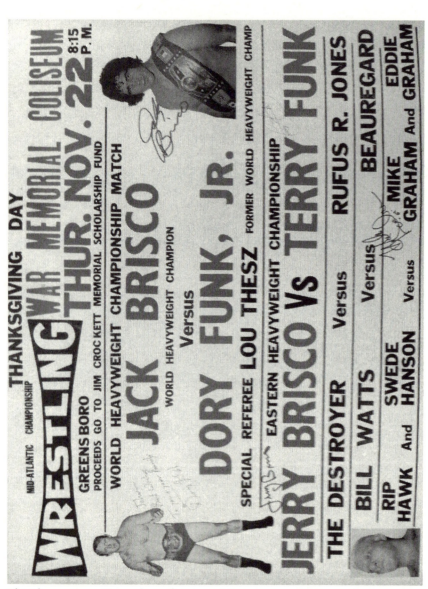

Florida comes to Greensboro for one night.

WRESTLING

WAR MEMORIAL COLISEUM
GREENSBORO

SUNDAY MAY 30
3:00 P.M.

TRIPLE MAIN EVENT

WORLD TITLE MATCH

TERRY FUNK
CHAMPION

Versus

DUSTY RHODES

U.S. TITLE MATCH

WAHOO McDANIEL
Vs
BLACKJACK MULLIGAN

GRUDGE MATCH

RUFUS R. JONES vs RIC FLAIR

JOHNNY WEAVER And TIGER CONWAY, JR.

MIDGET TAG TEAM MATCH

GEETO & BOLO MONGOL
Versus
LITTLE BROOK And LITTLE JIMMY

LORD LITTLE BROOK And LITTLE JIMMY Versus HAITI KID And LITTLE LOVE

EMANUEL SOTO v. SGT. JACQUES GOULET ★ ROBERTO SOTO v. MIKE "THE JUDGE" DUBOIS ★ MR. HAYASHI v. PETE SANCHEZ

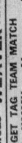
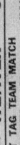

43

Stupid Old Lady

Another night of grappling, circa 1984.

I always cheered the heels, as you may know by now, and The Russians were one hot heel tag team in the '80s. Ivan Koloff, Crusher, and Nikita—the holy grail of communism—were on top of their game in the eighties and it took a brave soul to cheer for them.

The fans back then hated those guys with a passion, so I toyed with this hatred cautiously. On this night, I was sitting in the fourth row orange seats and realized that I was in a hot bed of redneck marks.

This can be dangerous if you show any fear, so I decided to be smart and observe these nuts before I started anything.

Turns out it was a family of idiot marks—a not so rare breed at this time. The loud-mouth mother, the cowardly father, and a few strange children. Classic material to play with.

So I start up with my Russian accent,

"I AM HEAR TO CHEER FOR MY UNCLE IVAN, COUSIN NIKITA, AND CRUSHER, THE ONLY SMART AMERICAN IN THIS STUPID COUNTRY!"

Suddenly the mother turns around and says, (I am not making this shit up!) "YOU ARE THE ONLY BASTARDS IN THIS PLACE CHEERING FOR THE GOD DAMN RUSSIANS!"

I replied, " I AM A VISITOR TO YOUR COUNTRY OLD LADY, WHY DO YOU TREAT ME SO RUDELY? I HAVE MY GREEN CARD AND WANT TO CHEER FOR MY FRIENDS AND FAMILY, WHAT IS YOUR PROBLEM? WHY DO YOU TREAT ME WITH LACK OF RESPECT?"

"I GOT A SON WHO IS FIGHTING A WAR AGAINST YOU COMMIE BASTARDS, AND I DO NOT LIKE YOU CHEERING FOR THEM!"

"WAR? WHAT WAR? A SECRET WAR? YOU ARE TOO STUPID TO HAVE FAMILY MEMBER IN THE C.I.A. SO SHUT UP OLD BITTER OLD LADY!"

The old lady kept pushing the same button. "I GOT A SON FIGHTING A WAR!"

"DO NOT WORRY OLD LADY, WHEN WE TAKE OVER YOUR STUPID COUNTRY WE WILL HAVE A JOB FOR YOU IN THE SALT MINES. YOU ARE A STUPID OLD LADY!"

I expected that the 'neck family would come to her defense by now but it seemed I was doing what the old man had wanted to do to her for years, he just sat there and quietly laughed. The kids got a chuckle too.

"I GOT A SON, WHO IS FIGHTING A WAR."

"AND DO NOT WORRY ABOUT YOUR PUPPET SON, I WILL KILL YOUR SON AND DANCE ON HIS GRAVE! I WILL DRINK A TOAST OF VODKA IN RED SQUARE TO YOUR STUPID SON, OLD LADY! YOU ARE A STUPID, STUPID IGNORANT OLD LADY! HAHAHAHAHA!!!"

A cheap shot but rule number one in heel fan survival, never back up once you go too far or you are in trouble. Any sign of weakness will get you a beat down, real fast. For the record, I am six foot two and a half and, at that time, about 225. You just keep going until the Marks retreat. The entire family did get up and leave after about 20 minutes with Old Lady screaming, "I GOT A SON (pant, pant,) WHO IS FIGHTING A WAR!"

"SHUT UP, STUPID OLD LADY!"

Those were the days, my friends, we thought they'd never end.

WRESTLING

WAR MEMORIAL COLISEUM

GREENSBORO

THUR. JUNE 8 8:15 P.M.

RETURN MATCH ★ NO DISQUALIFICATION

JOHNNY WEAVER

And

ART NELSON

Versus

RIP HAWK

& SWEDE HANSON

PLAYBOY GARY HART WILL BE HANDCUFFED TO THE ROPE

NELSON ROYAL

KLONDIKE BILL

Versus

OLE & GENE ANDERSON

LES THATCHER   And   **RONNY ETCHISON**

Versus

BILL BOWMAN   And   **JOE TURNER**

BY BRISCO v. ROCK HUNTER ★ SANDY SCOTT v. KRUSHER KARLSON ★ MATTI SUZUKI v. BOBBY WHITLO

47

The Devil's Triangle

It was time for a special Rasslin card in Greensboro, the first appearance of the Road Warriors in the heart of the Mid-Atlantic. They were going to defend the AWA belt against the NWA Champions, Dusty Rhodes and the Raging Bull, Manny Fernandez.

The Russian character I was portraying was just too good to give up. One night I got dressed up in a long green trench coat with a red KGB button. I played the insane Russian to the hilt, the few brave folks that came to the match with me got out of the way and let me go where I wanted.

I located the Stupid Old Lady in the cheap seats and waved to her. She gave me a hand gesture that was very warm; I was still Number One with her. "LOOK! THERE IS STUPID OLD LADY!"

As I made my way to my seat I goose stepped to the front. I couldn't believe how much heat was being generated by my appearance. Suddenly, another crazy lady went off on me from the second row. "Why are you cheering for the goddamn russkies?" Always remember: never break character and never show fear

I shot back, "I am here to cheer my family. Uncle Ivan, cousin Nikita!"

"You are the only person in this town that is cheering for the Russians!"

"You are wrong drunk old lady, there are many communists right here in your country."

"You are a damn lying bastard!"

Now I felt that maybe I might have gone a little to far but I figured I should make a grandstand play to get this nut off of my back. Notice I called the lady a nut and I am the one wearing a communist soldier uniform.

"I WILL PROVE TO YOU FOOLISH LADY THAT THERE ARE MANY WHO ARE SUPPORTERS OF MY CAUSE! WATCH AND SEE!"

I stood up and pointed to a group of heel fans to my right, I pointed for about ten seconds, and saluted arm across my chest towards them. I did not know these people but it was worth the gamble. Suddenly and shockingly the group of 15 people stood up and saluted back! Then I pointed to another group that my little brother Bob had brought with him and I saluted them. They all stood up and saluted back. Perfect.

I looked back at the woman and said, "You see old lady, Senator McCarthy was right, we are taking over your country!" That brought the house down. Even fans that hated me laughed at that one.

The main event was a wild one. The Road Warriors kicked the living shit out of Rhodes and Manny. I saw my first triple back-breaker that night and Tommy Young stopped the match on a lame count out. Amazing that the NWA Champs would get trashed in Greensboro.

A week or so later I met the leader of the first fan group that saluted, Dan Grondy and his group joined my small gathering and at the next show we started the 'Front Row.' Greensboro heel fans had a place to sit, a place to cheer, and a place to be themselves for the next eight years.

And remember the commie theme song to the tune of 'We Are The World'—"WE OWN THE WORLD! WE BEAT YOUR CHILDREN!"

Horsemen!

A magic night in Greensboro. For the first time an army of fans sitting together cheering for the heels. I had no idea just what was getting underway but this group consisted of about 12 obsessed fans that all wanted to have a great time.

In the group was Billy Pritchett, his brother Jimmy, Bud Grondy, Steve Stamper, Obin Johnson, Big Eddie, and yours truly. Walking across the arena floor Billy came running up to me with white tape on his nose—it was a jab at Ricky Morton and his famous broken nose angle.

That gained a lot of attention from the other fans, we were marked men. Before long every nose in our group was taped, we were all Rock and Roll haters. We had seats about eight rows up in the orange section. That put us in the middle of the action with walkways in front and behind us.

Remember, this was late 1985 and Marks ruled the earth. No one ever cheered the Heels in such a manner. It's hard to imagine wrestling before ECW but this activity was a lot more dangerous in practice than I ever thought possible. The fans came over in droves wanting a piece of us. The first was a grubby woman who asked, "Is that tape for the Rock and Roll or against them?"

We all went on the offensive. Remember, never show fear. Never.

"We are cheering for the Horsemen, real men. Not a bunch of pussy boys like Hoot and Punky! We are like Arn and Flair and Tully! We are only interested in the big girls in the sweaters! Not the little girls in the T-shirts and the training bras! Ole would kick you out of bed!"

The shit hit the fan!

All during the intermission people swarmed over to us to give us hell. And they never knew what was coming. We continued to talk the trash we had heard on TV, all the great lines from the Heel's interviews of the past. When I ran out of gas, Bud or Obin would jump right in

Folks thought that I could talk shit—well, Billy (PS) Pritchett was my equal and then some. Billy never ran out of gas, he was a freak of nature with a stunning voice like an ice pick being dragged loudly across a black board. "Rock and Roll? That's not Rock and Roll! Steppenwolf! That is real Rock and Roll!"

Suddenly a heavy chick showed up, pulled up her sweater and showed us her breasts!" Are these big enough?"

"If that's a hope chest, keep on hoping! If those are pancakes you better flip them." This other weird chick came by to read us a poem on why we were wrong and should be forgiven for our sins.

Then it got real strange.

They had another intermission. I have never seen this before but there was so much noise that the wrestlers were wandering out to see what was happening. I saw Ole and Barry Windum look around and laugh.

I was yelling at some fan or group of fans when a friend, Tarron Coalson, ran down to tell me if I need any help to let him know and he would help me fight my way out. I didn't know just what he was talking about until Dan Grondy showed up and said he'd help us get out as well.

"What do you mean Dan? We can handle a bunch of dumb ass fans!"

Dan looked me right in the face to get my attention and said, "Look around you and see what you are causing!"

I let Billy take over and looked around to see at least 400 fans surrounding our group. And they ain't happy. It was unbelievable. People were yelling and throwing popcorn and drinks at us. I got hit with three drinks and Stamper got hit with a spit cup. It was a madhouse!

Then I realized that the main event was Rock and Roll versus Flair and Tully Blanchard for the World Tag Team Belts. Flair was the World champ and Tully was the US Champ so there was no way that Flair and Tully

THE START OF THE FRONT ROW. 1985.   J. Hamilton

would win the straps. We were dead men.

Well, if you're going to die, go down fighting!

Thankfully it was time for the main event and Flair, Tully, and J.J. Dillon came out to the ring. Once they entered the ring, we all held-up the signs we brought that night.

Read together they said, in three-foot letters, HORSEMEN!

From the ring J.J. pointed out the signs to our champions and both stood and clapped for us. I never thought that we would be noticed like that. This was a first, no one had signs but us.

Then, on the count of three, we flipped our signs and they spelled out, ROMPEROOM.

Once again J.J. caught it first and showed the guys. Tully Blanchard laughed so hard that he sat on the second turnbuckle and pointed! Flair turned around to did his famous WHOOOO! while pointing and clapping for us. Ric Flair, our hero, clapping for us? What a moment.

Then the music started for the Rock and Roll express: Drummmma, Dummma druma druma, druma druma!

We turned the signs around to the Horsemen side as Ricky and Robert ran into the ring to a thunderous ovation. As they hit the ring Flair and Tully, hands on their hips, smiled and pointed out our HORSEMEN! sign.

That's when we turned them around to: ROMPEROOM. They looked like a couple of puppies hit with a newspaper.

We then started chanting," Broken Nose! Broken Nose!" and pointed to our taped noses. We all took a Pepsi bath on that one. The heat was brutal. So we began to plan our hasty escape.

But a miracle happened. As the match neared the finish, Tully grabbed a chair and wedged it between the top and middle ropes. Flair grabbed Little Rickey by the hair and the seat of his tights and rammed him head first into the chair .

And then he pinned him! ONE, TWO, THREE!

We celebrated like six year olds at Christmas! It was then announced by Doctor Tom Miller that it was a non-title match. They changed the match to save us! Or was it just luck? The fans just faded away into the night.

After the matches Jim Crockett, Jr. went to the dressing room to ask, "What was that Horsemen stuff?" Arn Anderson stated that he had referred to themselves as the Four Horsemen of the Apocalypse in an interview. "I guess those guys in the crowd picked up on it."

Crockett thought about it, "I think we should run with this Horsemen thing." And the rest is history.

I am honored! But there is no way on God's green earth that I am more annoying, arrogant, obnoxious or louder than the great John Hitchcock. As I recall that night over and over again (after reading John's representation of events) the one thing I really remember was that he was definitely getting the heat. I was there, and I was running my mouth, but damn, did they hate John. What a great memory.

- Billy PS Pritchett

I enjoy John Hitchcock's columns on the Front Row of the historic Greensboro Coliseum. I've heard comments that a lot of people are crying bullshit on the night of the Horseman. Since I was there, sitting in the back, I thought I would offer my opinion.

It was a big crowd, and the heat was tremendous. John and the and had a lot to do with it. The crowd was just as loud between matches as during matches, because that's when Front Row, Section D, would do their work. We were all concerned that the Front Row may be going too far, there were rows and rows of fans behind them yelling and screaming. When the main event was about to begin, John and his cronies held up the ROMPER ROOM signs, Rock N Roll were not happy and let John know it. Then the Heels came out. ROMPEROOM was flipped to HORSEMAN. Ole, Arn, Tully, and the Nature Boy turned their heads and covered their mouths, the universal wrestling sign for trying not to break character. It was an awesome night.

Should he take credit for the HORSEMAN? Maybe. Tully did give the Greensboro Crowd credit on a local radio show sometime in the nineties (Hey, I'm almost as old as John, give me a break.)

Is Billy "PS" Pritchett as annoying, arrogant, obnoxious or louder than John. Yes, Billy is John's equal in that regard.

-Dan Grondy

HORSEMEN! ROMPEROOM. 1985.   J. Hinn co/02

Free Cotton!

One odd night of rasslin occurred after I decided to go with a different group of fans. Simp, an old friend of my brother, gathered a bunch of crazy guys together to attend a match. Simp was a real piece of work, without a doubt the loudest man who ever walked the planet. One night he barked at Tommy Young for 45 minutes straight until Tommy stopped and asked me what was that guy drinking? If I could find out he wanted some.

Anyway, a night with Simp was a real treat. He had a new crew with him, one guy was really pounding down the Buds—before the show, in the parking lot, anywhere he could. All I remember was his name was Cotton and he was ready for Rasslin.

Funny, I cannot remember a single match that night. All I remember was Cotton screaming at the top of his lungs, and I quote, "THIS IS IT!" Cotton must have said that 75 times. Finally Simp asked him about it. Cotton grabbed the front railing and screamed, "THE GREENSBORO COLO IS TURNING OVER!"

I laughed so hard I am still hurting to this day.

We were sitting about 15 rows up when Cotton decided he wanted a piece of Greensboro's Finest. There was a really ugly female cop walking around keeping the peace. Suddenly, Cotton started yelling at her that she looked like Ester from Sanford and Son. He was just hammering this mean look-ing chick and finally she snapped and when after him!

Ester called over more cops to join the chase but Cotton somehow got away. He sneaked back to our group, then a redneck fan with his family started yelling for the cops.

Cotton ran like hell again but the police caught him at the escalator. He was screaming, "HELP! HELP! YOU GUYS HELP ME! HEY, GUYS, I WAS ONLY KIDDING! HELP!"

"GOD HELP ME!"

Funniest thing I ever saw.

But I was pissed at the neck family for squealing so I turned back and lit in to one of them. I called him a squealer. I called him a coward. I even told his family that their old man didn't have any guts! I challenged him to face me in a fight. He was so angry he got up and left the show.

For the record... Cotton was the first and last person that went to wrestling with me to spend the night in jail. Imagine trying to explain to his wife that he was arrested because of rasslin.

At his hearing the judge banned him for life from wrestling matches in Greensboro, ruling it was just too exciting for him to attend in person. No more live action for him.

What a way to go out.

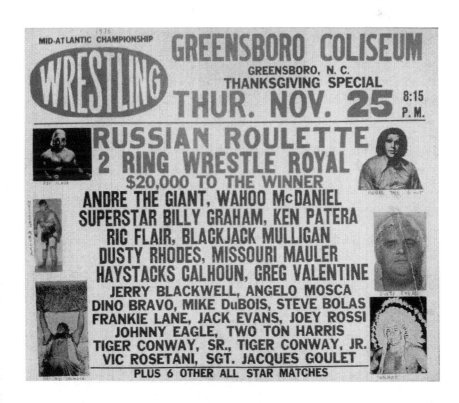

David Crockett, Five Cops and Dusty Rhodes

I started making signs and taking them to rasslin on a regular basis, I have a BFA in painting so they always stood out. One of the earlier efforts was a Nikita Koloff growth chart with a figure of Nikita indicating where the other good guys measured up to him.

This was a time when the Russians were the big heel trio and nobody cheered for these evil commies. Well, except my twisted friends and myself.

When I held up the chart, at the match Ivan and Nikita stopped and we got a pose; they loudly told everyone that we were, "good Americans." That's the kind of heat that gets you thrown drinks and chewing gum. Yes, gum. This one toothless old lady was chewing gum and then throwing it at me. She ruined a new pair of jeans that night.

On another night I made a sign with Dusty Rhodes depicted as the Michelin Man. Flair was competing against Rhodes when I held that one up Nature Boy lost it laughing. Dusty didn't think it was so funny, he tried to spit on the sign. He missed and I'm sure some poor woman is still trying to get that lugie out of her blouse.

The Dream was an easy target, he had absolutely no sense of humor. Well, none when it came to himself. When you think back on it, how did this fat ass ever become such a big star? I admit he was a great interview and had a strange charisma. But what a tub.

If you put this guy in any bar no chick would ever talk to him, he would be the lonely old fellow at the end

Since it was easy to get at Rhodes he would be our next target. I got friends to help construct the ultimate sign. This was the era of the little markers so it took three days. We spelled out, DUSTY SUCKS! It was beautiful, no doubt was going to bring the house down. We were pumped to see what the reaction would be.

Later that evening at the Greensboro Coliseum...

I was carrying in this huge stack of posters when I noticed something unusual; a group of Greensboro policemen were checking everyone for signs. It was unreal that this could happen but there they were inspecting everyone who walked in.

Approaching the front gate I heard a familiar voice yell out, "There he is!"

It was David Crockett. He had Doug Dillinger and five cops waiting on me. Crockett approached me angrily, "You are not bringing in any posters tonight. This is my show and you are not coming in with those damn posters." I tried to argue but to no avail. I had to hide them under a pine tree. From that point on, Dusty made my list.

I told all my pals inside that I was detained at the border by the cops.

WRESTLING
WAR MEMORIAL COLISEUM
GREENSBORO
SUN. SEPT. 7
7:00 P.M.

DOUBLE MAIN EVENT

U. S. HEAVYWEIGHT TITLE MATCH

JOHNNY VALENTINE
CHAMPION
Versus

DUSTY RHODES

TEXAS TORNADO ELIMINATION MATCH

OLE & GENE ANDERSON
Versus

PAUL JONES And WAHOO McDANIEL

KEN PATERA & R. JONES Vs **RUFUS R. JONES** Vs **MALENKO & MAULER**

GREAT MISSOURI Versus **SPOILER NO. 2**

TIM WOODS Versus BRUTE BERNARD

SWEDE HANSON Versus ART NELSON ★★ ★ Versus KLONDIKE BILL

TIGER CONWAY Versus DOUG GILBERT

CHARLIE FULTON And BILL HOWARD Versus GREG PETERSON And TONY ROCCA

Jimmy C and Captain Redneck

A key element of rasslin was the TV interview spaced between the matches, that extra push to entertain and provoke viewers to rush down and buy tickets to the live matches. To my friends and myself the interview was the funniest thing on television.

The Good Guys always seemed put off by this part of the act while the Bad Guys lived for it, Heels could almost always talk. It their job to rile viewers into hating them so much that they would boo the hell out of them in person.

But to me they were sending hidden messages. That's right, hidden messages.

We would fall out laughing at the rude, racist, or asshole things that they would say in these interviews. On the Front Row we played off of them constantly. It was like a game to see what grappler would get the biggest reaction in Greensboro. The Heels were smart enough to have noticed their loyal fan base. Pretty much just us. So they began telling us what they wanted to see, what would piss off the Babyfaces.

Jimmy Cornette was managing Captain Redneck Dick Murdock. Cornette gave an inspired performance in an interview where he stated that he went down to Texas, home of the American Dream Dusty Rhodes, to find out any information that would help Cappy Red defeat Rhodes.

Cornette said he looked high and low and found out that Dusty was not the son of a plumber as he claimed. Dusty's father was a cobbler. That's right, a cobbler. Because everywhere he went the people of Texas referred to Dusty's father as a black loafer.

I know, even then it was an old joke. But it gave me the secret message I was listening for—a poster guaranteed to get an explosive response.

Hours later at the Coliseum, right after Cornette and Dick Murdock made their entrance, I held up a sign with a drawing of a black shoe with 'Dusty's Father' written on it. Cornette almost fell down laughing but Murdock didn't get it, he looked confused when Cornette pointed it out.

The match was a squash and Captain Red Neck beat his opponent with a SIMPLE SIGNS CAN RULE THE WORLD. brain buster. I never did see brains busting out of somebody's head whenever they used that finishing move. We cheered like hell for Murdock who, I guess, got tired of being in the early matches so he grabbed the house mic and yelled out a challenge to Dusty.

Now this was a loud challenge, the Coliseum had just put in a new PA system. It was echoing off the ceiling as Murdock screamed for Rhodes. You already know how much I hated Rhodes so.... Billy, Bud and I started chanting, "DUSTY's YELLOW! DUSTY's YELLOW!"

All at once Dick Murdock stopped when heard us and said, "ALLLLL RIGHT!" Jumping from the ring he held the microphone right in front of us while we chanted, loud and clear out over the entire arena, five choruses of 'Dusty's Yellow!'

As Murdock began to pull the mic away I grabbed it and yelled as loud as I could, "AND HE SUCKS TOO!" I think that's when Cornette lost it. Rarely have I ever seen a real pro crack up like that. Murdock stood still, smiled and saluted us in classic Captain Redneck fashion.

At intermission I had to use the bathroom so what was in store for me was a little uncertain. I barely got out into the hallway before a bunch of fans began yelling at me, at least 7 or 8 guys all wanting a piece! This could get ugly fast. Naturally, some random insane lady also stepped into the fray to really get up into my face. "How dare you say anything bad about Dusty! He is the greatest wrestler in the world!"

I couldn't let that go. I responded," If Dusty is so tough why didn't he come out and FIGHT? What's a matter with him, he's not deaf? I think he didn't want any of BIG DICK! And I think that is your problem too, old lady! You are scared of BIG DICK!"

I quickly ducked into the rest room to escape the unruly mob. That wasn't my smartest move because now I was in close quarters and a few of the rabble followed and continued to harass me. When I stepped out of the bathroom only a handful remained to defend Dusty's honor. I beat a hasty retreat back to the Front Row where I took a drink shot to the back for my troubles. I stayed close the Front Row until the event was over. Then I ran like hell back to my car.

Every night when we left the arena we would agree that it couldn't get any better than that. And you know what?

It always did.

★ THE WORLD CUP OF ★

The
JIM
CROCKETT SR.
MEMORIAL
CUP

★ A PROFESSIONAL WRESTLING ★

April 22, 1988   Greenville, S.C.
April 23, 1988   Greensboro, N.C.

$4.00

The Crockett Cup and Big Nicky

This was a huge show for the Mid-Atlantic Territory and the Crockett's really did march out the top talent for this event. The deal was this was a tag team tournament for the Crockett Cup and a quote, a lot of cash, unquote. There was an early snag because a few of the teams I wanted to see were eliminated the night before in Greenville, South Carolina.. But anytime you can sit of the front row and watch the Midnight Express, Tully Blanchard, and Arn Anderson, The Road Warriors and the Fantastics you knew it was going to very entertaining night.

Well, Lex Luger and Sting won the Crockett Cup over Tully and Arn which proves there is no justice. It was a little shocking, that was the first time Tully and Arn ever lost a match in Greensboro. At least Dusty didn't win it again. But there was another match between Ric Flair versus Nikita Koloff.

Nikita was now a good guy teaming with his new friend Dusty Rhodes so we hated him. It was a Front Row heel turn and now Big Nicky was going to get some shit from us. It started kind of oddly, after a few power moves by Koloff the match settled into Flair working an arm bar on Koloff who lay on his stomach doing nothing. Yes, lying there like a dead fish. God, the match just started and Koloff went for a rest hold right out of the gate. I could not stand it and went off on him.

"How can you just lay there you lazy bastard! Flair could have a match with a broom stick but he can not carry your sorry ass! Get up and do something, you are boring us to tears. This show is on pay per view! Do something ya lazy bastard! How does it feel to be the worst wrestler in the world?"

That line did it.

All at once Big Nicky got up and basically threw Flair at us over the top rope! We knew this could get ugly fast. Koloff was about 285 pounds of muscle and was pissed. Roid Rage? Could be but he wanted a piece of my ass, that much was for sure. Koloff slammed Flair and started yelling at me. And I quote, "I suck? You suck, motherfucker!"

What was great was he yelled that in perfect Russian, staying in character. I was sitting as this monster just lost it and I said again, "How does it feel to be the worst wrestler in the fucking world! You really do suck!"

"Fuck you!" Koloff puppy pumped right in front of me. I lost it too, as he turned to get back in the ring I gave him the finger.

Where was Flair? Well, he was crawling on the floor laughing his ass off at the whole thing. Glad I gave him so much enjoyment but I was kind of shaken. Koloff won the match on a DQ finish but Flair kept the title.

If you watch the tape of this show, Crockett Cup 1988, watch for that moment. The camera catches only a little of this confrontation but you can see Flair laughing and Nikita crotch thrusting in my direction. Jackie Crockett was really on the ball and captured very little of this drama on the actual broadcast.

Damn him.

Grandma

"How the hell did you get those tickets on the Front Row every time?" A question posed to us by Marie Brown, known as Grandma to the Front Row faithful. And she helped us get them.

We went to every Crockett show in 1985. And I mean every show. In fact, we went to anything with a ring and chairs. It became very important for our physical safety, however, to sit on the front row. There were security guards at ringside, we had to be as close as possible. I use to get to the ticket booth at seven in the morning for those choice seats. On many, many occasions the best I could get was second row.

That really pissed me off. Imagine being the first in line, every time, and getting second row. I lost it on one occasion, yelling that the world is not fair, we waited, we paid our dues, we sacrificed for the show, this was a grave injustice us settling for second row.

Yeah, I am a spoiled pussy.

Later in the week, at an independent show, a nice old dame walked up to me and asked if I was able to get the tickets I wanted for the last Coliseum event. I said no, it was so unfair waiting for three hours, first in line, only to get lousy seats. She told me she had an 'in' that could solve our problem.

The deal was we had to pay for the show in advance to get the Front Row seats. Needless to say I was thrilled and gave her some money to start the ball rolling. By coincidence another couple of guys that had suffered with me waiting at the ticket booth were at that show and I brought them into the mix.

Those two guys were Obin Johnson and Big Eddie who became Front Row stalwarts from then on.

So, who is Marie Brown? A wonderful person from the old school of professional wrestling. The stories she could tell. She used to attend matches in the forties held on top of the YMCA long before the Greensboro Coliseum was built. She remembers all the classic wrestlers, hell she knew most of them.

She was there the night the Becker Brothers, George and Bobby, fought their last match. The brothers were the top face team for many years, although Bobby Becker had been diagnosed with terminal cancer he continued to wrestle. It's what he loved to do. Honestly, the only thing he could do. During that last match Bobby went up for a body slam and did not get back up. He died in the ring.

Later George Becker would tag with a young lion named Johnny Weaver and dominate the Mid-Atlantic scene for decades.

Grandma was there the night Luther Lindsay died in the ring as well. Lindsay was the first big breakthrough black star and it was terrible news when that happened. Grandma even has one of Homer O'Dell's canes!

She was at every big match in Greensboro history. Every one. You name it; she was witness to it all.

Stunning. And Marie Brown is still alive and as feisty as ever.

We all owe you one Grandma.

The People's Money

This promised to be another blockbuster night at the Coliseum—the return of Magnum TA.

For you young wrestling fans Magnum was, in real life, Terry Allen. That is where the TA came from. His character was modeled after the 1970s detective show, Magnum PI, he even had the cheesy mustache and haircut. Magnum had been the young top face in the Mid-Atlantic Promotion for years. A close friend of the American Dream, Dusty Rhodes, Magnum was a tall, tan superhero that every girl with a pulse and no brain could fall for.

"Magnum" T.A.

And of course, I hated him, typical good guy with little talent that was force fed down everyone's throat. He was so hot with the fans that Rhodes, to keep himself on top, made sure he was always by his side. Older wrestlers would always cling to the young up and comers to maintain their heat and keep their positions. Rhodes was the booker and had the power to do that; after years and years of abuse it hurt the promotion long term.

The classic Magnum match was usually 30 seconds finishing with the belly-to-belly suplex for the win. Time after time the same simple match—this drove me crazy. Couldn't the simple-minded fans see he was a lazy bum? I mean, he put no effort into his matches; he cheated the fans with these quick, mailed-in efforts. But that is what Dusty wanted.

On October 14, 1986 Magnum was involved in a brutal car wreck. This was huge, front-page headlines in the Greensboro and Charlotte newspapers. He was leaving a bar one night and lost control of the car. Many suspected he whad been drinking but that was never made public to protect Magnum's character and possible earnings. That didn't become an issue but he was left paralyzed on his right side, unable to wrestle.

The storyline for Magnum's return to the Coliseum fed off Dusty's feud with Tully Blanchard, the current US Champion. Dusty put up $10,000 of his own money to guarantee the match would take place. Dusty asked his pal Magnum to be there for support and to hold the "Peoples Money."

That is what they called it, the "People's Money," It may well have been the people's money. I spent enough of it going to these damn shows, so I guess it was.

The night of the match out comes Magnum in a golf cart to a standing ovation of about 9,000 people. It was not a sellout though, people forget their heroes quickly when they aren't on television anymore.

We all stood and as the crowd began to quiet, I began to sing the TV jingle, "Don't drive drunk! Do da do do to ad do do." Stevie Wonder sang this on a commercial to warn people to drive responsibly and it seemed appropriate.

Believe it or not, Magnum smiled and shook his head grinning.

Anyway, the match got underway with Dusty kicking Tully all over the ring. Dusty was all offense for three fourths of the match. Magnum even tripped Tully during the match to a huge roar from the crowd. Tully's manager JJ Dillon was visibly worried at ringside as Rhodes continued to destroy Tully.

Against all odds, Tully was going to win this match. The old school rule of booking was the guy who takes the beating wins the match. After all, he's doing all the work. If it was a Dusty Rhodes' match, however, everybody else did all the work. Rhodes could hardly walk much less wrestle. Without a doubt, Dusty was the most out of shape wrestler in the business.

Well, that's not fair. Abdulla the Butcher was much fatter than Rhodes but that was his job to be obese and scary. Rhoades was just plain fat. Come to think about it, he was real scary too.

As match wore on the heat in the arena was amazing. People were going nuts for the Dream. And Tully was selling like few in the business could.

I do want you folks to know that Tully Blanchard was one of the best wrestlers I have ever seen in person. He was born into a wrestling family and knew the ring like most of us know our living room. He rarely made a mistake and was rarely out of position. He is as great an athlete as the sport ever witnessed. I would rank Flair, Terry Funk and Tully Blanchard as the best I have ever seen in the ring.

At the finish of the match, all looked bad for Tully when he was hit with the Atomic Elbow and pinned. Right after the three count, Tully placed his foot on the rope.

Dusty exploded in celebration as J.J. took the "Peoples Money" from Magnum and ran away with it. Rhodes jumped out of the ring and began to chase after J.J. in a wild pursuit. During this some crazy fan ran down to ringside and yelled out, "Stop him! He has got the Peoples Money! J.J. Dillon has the Peoples Money!" I will never forget this guys face. He believed this stuff completely.

Now... about that foot on the ropes. We began to scream to Tommy Young that Tully had his foot on the ropes during the count of three. And believe it or not Tommy Young paid attention to us!

Obin Johnson and myself put our legs on the top of the front railing and began to plead with the referee to re- start the match. Here we are yelling for justice with our legs on the rail. "You got to do it Tommy!"

"It is the right thing to do!"

And you know what? He changed the finish and re-started the match! Dusty was out in back of the arena chasing down J.J. and didn't hear the count. The American Dream was defeated and lost the Peoples Money.

A sense of justice had finally come to Greensboro. Now this made fans wonder. Was all this planned and we were unknowingly used to create the finish? I always felt that way, everyone knew the reaction that finish would get from us. If you ever see a video of this classic match, look for Obin and me on the Front Row with our legs on the railing.

Aaah, wrestling is what made America great...

MID-ATLANTIC CHAMPIONSHIP

WRESTLING

"AIR CONDITIONED"

WAR MEMORIAL COLISEUM

GREENSBORO

THUR. JULY 26 8:15 P. M.

DOUBLE MAIN EVENT

EASTERN HEAVYWEIGHT CHAMPIONSHIP

THUNDERBOLT PATTERSON

IF PATTERSON LOSES HE FORFIETS $3,000 TO ANDERSON

Versus

JERRY BRISCO

Versus

GENE ANDERSON

IF ANDERSON LOSES HE MUST TAKE OFF THE GLOVE HE HAS BEEN ALLOWED TO WEAR

OLE ANDERSON

ROYAL KANGAROOS

Versus

AMAZING ZUMA And BEAUREGARD

GIRLS! PENNY BANNER Versus BELLE STARR

COWBOY BILL WATTS Versus LUMBERJACK DUPREE

BOB ROOP Versus TONY ROMANO

JOHNNY RINGO ★ EL GAUCHO Versus LES THATCHER

BRUTE BERNARD Versus

Doctor Tom Miller

Dr. Tom Miller was the ring announcer at the Greensboro Coliseum and was one of the finest ring announcers I can remember; he took over for the legendary Wally Dusiek who still walked to ring side acting as a timekeeper.

I guess that is what Wally did, anyway. I suppose he was the guy who wouldn't go home. He could barely walk or see but he was always in attendance. Dr. Tom was a subtle face announcer who always seemed to dislike the heels. He was a booming presence and when he and Wally went to the ring, you knew the show was about to begin.

After the show, the Front Row Crew usually went to Shoney's for dinner. The food was good and cheap and they stayed open late. The place was always packed after Wrestling so we would get there as soon as possible and grab a big table.

One night, Dr. Tom and his son showed up. I asked him to sit with us and he did. This was a surprise because it was the first time that a professional ever sat down with us and talked. But it was a choice between sitting with us or a long wait, so we got lucky.

Dr. Tom was a large guy at least 375 pounds so I always felt he could take care of himself. He had a radio show for years as 'Trucker Tom,' he was a good man and easy to talk to. He didn't open up easily but as time went on he could tell we loved Wrestling so everything was cool. He got friendlier and answered all our questions, he knew us anyway from the signs we brought to show after show.

Soon the stories began to flow. This was before the newsletters so this was new ground for us.

The show we had just attended was the big UWF / NWA show and it was a hot one. It was the first time we got a look at the Freebirds, Doctor Death Steve Williams, Chris Adams, Sting, Rick Steiner, etc.

It was a great time to be a wrestling fan and the first question was about all the possible match ups with these two groups combining. Dr Tom said flatly that by the first of the year there would be no UWF—that both groups would become one. That really sucked and I went off on the loss of the good feuds, teams fighting for their group, etc. No dice, we were informed that Crockett was ending UWF.. In hindsight this was one of the many blunders that Crockett Promotions would make that eventually caused them to sell the promotion to Ted Turner.

Then the topic of the signs came up and Dr Tom said that the two people that we blew out the most deserved it. "Ricky Morton is a smart ass punk. And Jimmy Garvin thinks he is a better wrestler than Ric Flair!"

"Whatever you do, keep giving it to them, they deserve it!"

"All the guys love you. So keep it up," he told us.

"What about Dusty?" I asked.

"You don't understand, Dusty is the trail boss. He tells people who is going to win and who is going to lose. He's the booker and has power over everyone. So when you stick it to him, you're doing just what all the guys wish they could do."

Dr. Tom was into his spaghetti when I asked what Dusty thought about the signs. He stopped eating, raised his fork, pointed it at me and said, "He hates you! He hates your guts!"

I said, "Good! I hate him too."

"No, you do not understand. He really hates you. All I can tell you is, you better not get caught in a dark alley with Rhodes. He would kill you! And he is a dangerous man. I am not telling you to stop, by all means keep doing it because it raises the Boy's spirits.

But be careful around Dusty." We had many more nice meals and chats, it became one of my favorite parts of wrestling, meeting with Dr. Tom and his son.

Dr. Tom Miller passed away a long time ago; wrestling was never the same for me. So now you know. Dr. Tom was Deep Throat.

Mad Dog

Every generation there are a few guys that are one of a kind naturals. By that I mean the rare breed that you have never seen anything like, before of after.

That is Buzz Sawyer to me.

Sawyer was a once in a lifetime athlete, a physical force of nature with brilliant strength, timing, and was totally fearless in the ring. Now everyone will tell you Sawyer was not a nice guy. Matter of fact, he hurt a lot of wrestlers and didn't seem to care.

I am not talking about the Buzz Sawyer who screwed somebody out of their training money. The guy I am talking about dominated the Georgia Territory along with Wrestling Two, Tommy Rich, The Masked Superstar and Ole Anderson. Every week on TBS for two hours Buzz Sawyer would just kick the shit out of people. His power slam was his finisher, he defied gravity jacking guys up and powering them to the mat.

His interviews were incredible, he would rant and scream at Gordon Solie with such force he would start to foam at the mouth.

One day in Greensboro I was very pleased to see Sawyer walking into the building to wrestle that night. Didn't have a clue he was going to be on the card but I could not wait to finally see him in action. The match was Buzz vs the Ever Popular Johnny Weaver who, as you now know, was the local legend. There was no way Sawyer knew what he was in for.

You could tell nobody in the backroom tipped Buzz off that he was to take it easy on the guy who was hanging on for a check.

Sawyer suddenly ate Weaver up like a hungry lion in with a lamb and Buzz sold very very little for The Weave. The match broke down like this. Sawyer launched Weaver off the ropes into a forearm smash that knocked Weaver silly. Sawyer then tossed Weaver over the top rope. He took an awkward fall but Sawyer jumped out after him, scooped him up and dropped him knee first on the wooden ring steps. The only way to describe this was painfully brutal. Sawyer just dropped Weaver with all his weight right on the steps with an atomic knee drop move. The referee ran down to

Weavers' aid and asked him if he was OK.

Weaver told the ref, "Get me out of here this guy is a madman."
Sawyer grabbed up Weaver, tossed him into the ring, then threw Weaver
off the ropes for his legendary Power Slam. Weaver limped to the Slam
then Sawyer jackhammered the poor guy for a quick pin.

It was nasty as referee, Tommy Young put his arm around Weaver and
helped him to the back. Weaver was limping very badly.

With in a few weeks Johnny Weaver was announcing the matches, doing
the color with Bob Caudle, and no longer in the ring. Buzz Sawyer soon
went back to Georgia to wrestle.

I guess if you retire a legend, well, you've got to go too.

ONE OF THE GREAT CHAIRSHOT ARTISTS OF ALL TIME!

HARDCORE

BY: JOHN "I GOT THIS STORY FROM HARRY NICHOLS" HITCHCOCK '9

BACK IN THE OLD MID ATLANTIC NWA DAYS, T.V. TAPING WAS AT CHANNEL 5 IN RALEIGH N.C. OH, ABOUT 1977-78? I GUESS.

AN OLD FRIEND HARRY WENT TO THE WEDNESDAY NIGHT TAPINGS AND AFTERWARDS WENT ACROSS THE STREET TO A BAR..

A BAR, BAR.. OK?

WHEN THEY WENT IN WHO'S THERE BUT WAHOO, PAUL JONES AND THE LEGEND HIMSELF ANDRE THE GIANT.

HARRY IS A SUPER NICE AND BRAVE GUY INTRODUCED HIMSELF AND CUT UP SOME WITH THE CROP GUYS. EVERYTHING WAS REAL COOL.

ANDRE WAS POUNDING DOWN SOME BEERS AND HAVING A GREAT TIME. HE TOOK OFF ONE OF HIS RINGS AND HARRY SWEARS HE COULD HAVE WORN IT LIKE A BRACELET.

AFTER ABOUT 30 MINUTES, ANDRE DECIDES TO TAKE A LEAK, AND AS ANY FUTURE JOURNALIST HARRY FOLLOWED. AFTER ALL WOULDN'T YOU?

NOW PICTURE THIS ANDRE DRAINING IT AND 5'6" HARRY CLIMBING UP ON THE TOILET IN THE NEXT STALL PEERING AT "THE GIANT"! HARRY SAID IF ANYONE EVER NEEDS A VIEN FOR A HEART TRANSPLANT CALL ANDRE!

ANDRE DID LOOK UP AT HARRY (MAKE THAT LOOK ACROSS AND SAID THE FAMOUS PHRASE "DO YOU WANT TO SEE THE GIANTS **DICK?**" NEEDLESS TO SAY HARRY RAN LIKE HELL!

OH GOD!

PISSSSSSS PISSSSSS

LATER ANDRE WENT OUT OF CONTROL AND STARTED YELLING "DO YOU THINK I AM A **FREAK?**" IT WAS ALL WAHOO AND P.J. COULD DO TO CONTROL HIM!

CHILL OUT FREAK MAN.

CRAZY SHIT MAN!

NOW THAT ANDRE HAS PASSED AWAY, I CAN'T HELP BUT REMEMBER THIS PICK-UP LINE! I WISH I COULD USE IT... DAMN IT! REST IN PEACE BIG MAN.

WRESTLING

<small>MID-ATLANTIC CHAMPIONSHIP</small>

GREENSBORO COLISEUM

GREENSBORO, N.C.

SUN. JULY 3

7:30 P. M.

MID-ATLANTIC TITLE MATCH

GREG VALENTINE
Vs
WAHOO McDANIEL
CHAMPION

ANDRE THE GIANT & MIGHTY IGOR
Versus
SUPER STAR & BLACKJACK MULLIGAN

RIC FLAIR   Versus   RICKY STEAMBOAT

KIM DUK And MISSOURI MAULER   Versus   BOBO BRAZIL And TIGER CONWAY

vs BRUTE BERNARD ★ MR. X vs STEVE KOVACKS ★ JERRY BLACKWELL vs DANNY MILLER

JOHNNY WEAVER

79

Mister Bruce

It is time to talk about the members of the Front Row.

I first met Bruce Mitchell in 1985 at the comic book store I was working for. This was the old Acme Comics in downtown Greensboro, a local hang-out where I met a lot of wrestling fans.

I guess I was the loudest guy many fans had ever met. I was always talking about wrestling and attended all the shows. One day this skinny guy kept jumping into my conversations, asking questions about who did what and how I knew about that. This square was wearing a Duke sweatshirt, I had never seen one before, so I figured he was either misguided or retarded so I was nice and answered all his questions.

Every week or so this same person would show up to buy comics and talk wrestling so a friend was made. It turns out this poor fellow was living in Oxford and then moved to Beckley, West Virginia, he was driving down every week to talk graps. Some people are a lonesome lot so we kept up the talk always about Mid-Atlantic Wrestling. Bruce was really dying to sit on the front row. Any front row. He had never sat that close before so I got him a ticket.

Well, here we are at Wrestling night and Bruce comes strolling in dressed in a suit. He was managing a Belk's store and drove 4 hours one way from West Virginia but didn't have time to change. I now knew he was really a fan.

Bruce was blown away by the hard-hitting action. Front Row Section D was the place to be, Wrestlers really loved the fans and the signs and, man oh man, did we get great matches every night, probably the best performances on the tour.

Bruce turns and asks me, "Can the wrestlers hear you when you yell at them?" I said why don't you try it and find out. You see, Bruce did not know that the match was the Rock and Roll Express and I had been giving Ricky Morton and Robert Gibson shit for years.

Those guys were THE hot faces in the promotion and were not used to being cheered against—it was the wrong thing to do. But a guy has to get experience in life somehow... so I let him have his moment with the R and R. Bruce stood up and yelled, "Hey Morton! You suck!"

A great moment in wrestling history, folks. Bruce Mitchell learning the realities of the Front Row. Man, was the Rock and Roll waiting for that one!

Ricky Morton runs across the ring like a madman and yells at the top of his lungs, "Hey Four Eyes! I have turned down more pussy in one day than you will get in your whole fucking life!"

Bruce is now the deer caught in the headlights and he froze totally shocked at the heated reaction. What Morton said was true. Hey, It was true with anyone in that business but that was not the issue.

Morton was attacking the Front Row and I could not stand for it. So I yelled back, "Hey Morton! Are we talking legal pussy here or any under aged teenyboppers in T-shirts and training bras or any farm animals you might have banged on the way here?"

Morton went nuts. Gibson even said something over that one. This was rare because I could never tell where that guy was looking.

Bruce just turned, sat down and looked at me and said, "Man, he really hates you!"

"Wait until you see Dusty," I said.

The rest of the time Morton ignored the match and yelled bloody murder at us and we loved every minute of it. After that Bruce never missed a show, he moved to Greensboro. I think it was because of the wrestling. He would say a teaching job and the ACC Basketball. Being the center of the universe, who are you going to believe?

The Front Row really started to take hold with more of a regular cast of characters. Obin, Big Eddie, Bruce, KC O'Connor, Russ, Angie, Lisa, Bud, Cheryl, Diamond Dan, Stamper, Harry, Doug and a few others. This crew was the solid Front Row Section D that became a Crockett TV backdrop for the next 6 years.

Two Ton

George 'Two Ton' Harris was one of my favorite guilty pleasures and only old time fans even know who he was. But that is true of all the old timers these days, only old farts like me remember them.

Two Ton was one of the reasons for my realizing that Pro Wrestling was a show. It became apparent to me in the fifth grade that Two Ton's matches were always the same routine.

If you had seen one match well, you had seen them all but I would not have missed them for the world. Two Ton always wore the same dark blue body suit to make him look smaller, I guess. His matches always started with the classic Wally Dusek introduction. "Ladies and Gentlemen"— pause three seconds, "From Louisville" (That's a guess), pause three seconds, "302 pounds," pause three seconds,

" George,

"Two Ton,

"Haaaaaarrisssss!"

Two Ton would be smiling in his ring corner, running his fingers through his curly hair. What a vain guy. After his name was spoken, he would stride out to the center of the ring to a chorus of boos and say, "SHUT AAP!"

Two Ton always lost the match and whenever he would put an opponent in a headlock, he would yell out for all to hear, "I GOT HIM NOW!" (This was said very quickly.)

With this happening every match even I began to believe that wrestling must be fixed or fake. Or both. (Except for the main events because those grapplers really did not like each other.)

Two Ton had a run as manager in the Mid-Atlantic, too. He was the manager of Aldo Bogni and Bronco Lubich. I guess he got this job because Homer O' Dell got fired or something.

I wish that I had known Two Ton's phone number when Scott

Hudson and Steve Prazak stopped by Greensboro to talk Graps. We were discussing our favorite wrestlers, jobbers and matches at a local Mexican restaurant when Steve started talking about Two Ton.

I said I could do an impersonation of him and did the "Shut Aaap!" It was that or my Lord Littlebrook that brought the house down! There was not a dry eye in the house that night. George Harris would have loved it.

I did get to see Two Ton Harris once. At one of the big Greensboro cards, they were putting up the cage and out comes Klondike Bill and his ring crew. And I could not believe it, out came Two Ton! He was part of the ring crew! I went nuts and told everyone who he was. Sadly few remembered him by the mid-1980s.

But as he walked past I said, "George

"Two Ton,

"Haaaaaarrisssss!"

He stopped for a moment then kept walking with the crew. But he knew someone remembered him. As the ring crew left the ringside he walked up to Klondike Bill and said something about my intro to him and they laughed. I hope he got a thrill out of that half as much as he gave me.

These forgotten stars are passing now and it seems so unfair that they did not receive cash value equal to the memories that they left behind.

They all would be very wealthy men now.

Remembering Tim Woods

Whenever I think about Tim Woods I think of that great pin move with the Three Quarter Nelson when he would wrap the guy up and be standing on his head. No one else ever did that move, it was his trademark finisher.

This move really pushed the amateur background of Woods. He would come to an area with his Pan Am Metals and really get over that legit aspect. Woods was tall about 6' 2" and could really move in the ring.

Woods came back to the Mid-Atlantic in a surprise move to challenge Johnny Valentine for his 1000 silver dollars, a TV match that ended with Johnny Valentine breaking Woods leg.

It was one of those scary moments were Valentine stood over Woods that got Johnny V over as a killer. As Woods lay in the ring, Valentine was interviewed and said that was going to happen to anyone that attempted to embarrass him. This kind of brutal angle was used later with Greg and Wahoo and we all remember that one.

I met Woods at the Grady Cole Center, the show that Jim Cornette set up. A lot of old hands were there. Swede, Woods, Scott, Weaver, Nelson Royal, Abe Jacobs, Magnum. Sadly, it was not that well attended. Partly because Smokey Mountain Wrestling was just starting to be seen in the Carolinas.

Tim Woods was about 350lbs at that time but he was a very nice guy. He signed my posters and would talk about the old days. Those old guys really loved being together on that day and I was really thrilled to meet my childhood idols.

Goofy Jimmy Garvin

I was a big fan of Jimmy Garvin in the World Class and AWA days, he was a great guy on the stick and his interviews made me laugh. I somehow never noticed that he sucked in the ring but it became very apparent when you saw the guy in person. He was without a doubt the laziest wrestler in the world.

I attended to a card in Winston Salem where Garvin was second from the top against the Warlord. Now, the Warlord was a huge steroid guy that did

not work well with others. Crockett Promotions always hid the big stiff in tag matches so Garvin was not wrestling anyone that was very good.

I understood from the beginning that it was going to be a challenge to enjoy a great match—a miracle if it would even be watchable. But being second from the top of the card there was that potential.

The match lasted all of 12 seconds! That is right. 12 SECONDS. The Warlord charged Garvin at the turnbuckle. Garvin stepped out of the way, Warlord hit the turnbuckle, then Garvin rolled him up for the pin.

That was a religious moment for me. Garvin mailed it in and went home that night not caring for one moment about the fans that paid to see him. From then on... he was on my list.

The list is a bad place to be because it meant you got the treatment from the Greensboro Front Row fans. And if you'll remember, Dr. Tom Miller had already informed me the guy was a pain.

One night I'm attending a match in Greensboro, Front Row of course, and out strolls Jimmy Garvin with his valet Precious (Garvin's real life wife) who had never been a big fan of the Front Row. Maybe it was the fact we would roll out dimes and nickels and ask her to pick them up? She carried a can of air freshener and sprayed it all around the ring just to piss off the fans. Bruce said he thought it was for some kind of itch problem.

Garvin's opponent was Tully Blanchard, one of the greatest wrestlers I personally have ever witnessed. Blanchard must have pissed off the management to be placed in an early match with Garvin because everyone knew Garvin was all show and zero in the ring.

I held up a sign that read, "GOOFY JIMMY" and Garvin and his wife went nuts. It always amazed me that the simple signs always got the best reaction. Tully loved it of course.

As the match began, Garvin basically chased Tully around the ring. As Garvin ran past Dr. Tom Miller he grabbed the announcer's drink to continue the chase. Just as he rounded the corner in front of me, Garvin threw the drink, missing Blanchard but flinging it right at the Front Row.

It was a setup to get even for the Goofy Jimmy sign. We didn't get too wet but there was a lot of ice at our feet while Garvin and

Precious laughed right at us.

Well, the one thing they did not count on was how much Tully Blanchard liked his Front Row Fans. We were the Original Horsemen Fans—Tully, Arn Anderson, and many other wrestlers would go on TV and talk about what we did that week and what signs we displayed. Tully once called Greensboro "The Home Court of the Horsemen." We loved those guys.

Anyway, I went crazy over Goofy Jimmy's attack against us and demanded that Tully get Garvin back. Along with Billy Pritchett I stood at the metal ring barrier, we had our drinks up, yelling for Tully to revenge us. I was hoping Tully would run by and grab my drink and toss it at Garvin.

Instead, Tully threw Garvin over the tope rope right at us! They were brawling outside the ring, getting closer and closer. In one quick move Tully winked at me as if to say, "Here he comes!"

Tully grabbed Garvin by the hair and slammed him across the ring barrier. At the exact same time as Garvin went down I went up with my drink, right into his head. It was perfect timing, the cup exploded, ice and cola went everywhere and I heard Garvin say—and I quote—"SHIT!"

I had done the one thing that Garvin wanted, a move that could finally get me kicked out of the Coliseum. for good What a fool I was! Finally the Garvins were going to see my big ass tossed to the curb for throwing a drink on a wrestler.

Then a miracle happened. Before police could grab me the Greensboro Coliseum Security got to me first and yelled for me to quit causing trouble and sit down. The group of Greensboro's Finest turned and just walked away, allowing security to handle the situation.

I lived to see another front row. Garvin could not believe it.

Now I could yell at him about how I got to cup him because he sucks— and everybody knows it. "Even the cops let me cup you because you suck!"
.

The Brute!

When I was a kid growing up with the mighty Mid-Atlantic you could tell if someone was a true wrestling fan very easily. Even if they were not die-hard fans they still had a Brute Bernard impression. Working at Food World in the early seventies I was unloading a truck one afternoon. This old driver suddenly breaks into the walk. He started to move in a short circle and wave his arms like a chicken. While he did this he said, "Oooo, Oooo, Ooo."

Then he stopped, looked skyward and yelled, "OooOOOooohhhh!" That's the Brute Bernard Shuffle. Everyone within earshot would do the same impression then start laughing.

Before Flair's "Whooo" there was The Brute. He was one of a kind. When I started watching television wrestling Brute Bernard and Skull Murphy were the first team that really stood out. Skull Murphy was a real intense interview, the leader and controlling force of this team. Brute Bernard was the animal that stalked around ringside scaring everyone. And I mean terrifying. Everyone believed this guy was totally nuts and it pushed The Skulls to the top.

When Skull Murphy died every fan was worried about what would happen to the Brute. I know I thought about it, Murphy was the controller of this mad beast. Who would get him food? How would he pay his bills? As a single, would the chicks still dig him?

Fans were told that Skull Murphy had passed due to a heart attack. A believable explanation but in reality he committed suicide. (Why? Who really knows about that kind of thing.)

Soon after, the Brute began to tag with the Missouri Mauler. This was a positive because even as the bad guys at least the Brute had someone to care for him. These kind of things really mattered when you were about ten years old.

The Mauler and Brute became big time main event wrestlers in the Mid-Atlantic. Interviewer Charlie Harville asked the Mauler if he could control

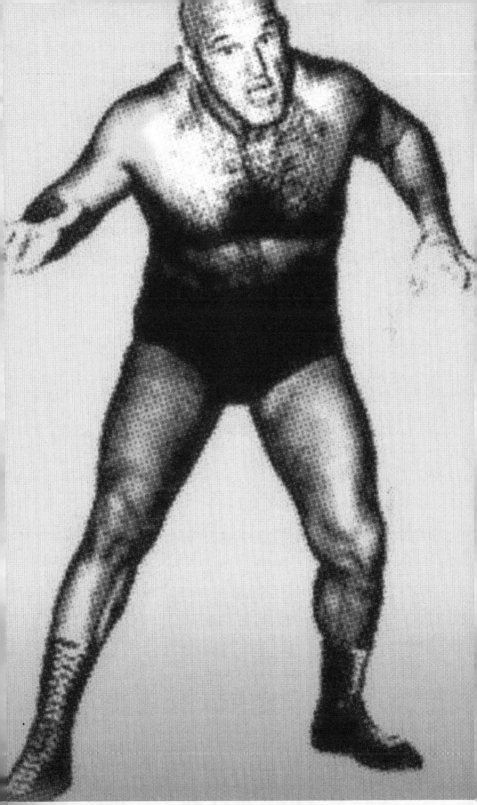

this man. The answer was, "What do you mean? If I had a son, I would want him to be just like Brute Bernard!"

The camera then took a shot of The Brute as he stood there drooling all over himself. It was a classic wrestling moment that few will ever forget.

One night the Brute was wrestling Number One Paul Jones. He had Jones in a front face lock and began to scream in his own unusual way. As he held the hold Brute began to drool. It wasn't any old drool, this was a white, 'I got a bad cold' kind of drool and Paul Jones saw it coming! This was the most punishing time consuming thing I ever remember watching on TV.

This snotty mess ran out of Brute's mouth and began to fall right down into Paul Jones face. As it got closer, you could see Paul Jones struggling to escape this fate worse than death. No dice, The Brute continued to yell and drool until it ran all over Jones' face. And man, Number One was not a happy camper.

I have lots of Brute Bernard stories.

What ever happened to Brute Bernard? Well, he got dropped from Crockett because he was too old to continue exerting himself that way. He then went over to the independents, working all around the Mid-Atlantic territory picking up a match whenever he could. There is one thing that I do know, Brute Bernard loved the sport. It was his life and, really, when you think about it, what else could a guy like that do?

One night working for Johnny Hunter the Brute snapped. The ref Dave Routh had no choice but to do a double count out finish that was not planned. The Brute was fighting on the floor and wouldn't get back in the ring. It was a mess and Routh did the right thing. After the match, Brute ran back to the dressing room and hit Routh, breaking his nose.

He was raising hell about being counted out and was totally out of control. Hunter had no choice but to fire him on the spot. When the reality sank in that Brute could no longer make a living wrestling, he broke down and started to cry.

A few months later, Brute Bernard went hunting with a few green kids. Suddenly Brute said, "Hey, you want to really see something?" Brute Bernard then raised his gun and shot himself in the head. The guys that were there couldn't do a thing to help him. They were too far away to get help there in time.

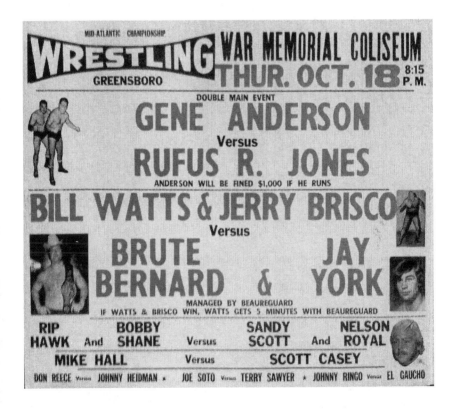

Johnny the Champ

Johnny Valentine was the wrestler that made it all real for me. His matches were stiff and brutal affairs and anyone who saw him live, never, and I mean NEVER, forgot him. My first time was on cable television, I think it from Florida about 1970-71, Valentine appeared in this territory for about a month. Within this short time frame he would have some intense, hard-hitting matches, break somebody's leg, then get suspended for life from the territory. I wondered if this guy was all business, that nobody wanted to wrestle him.

I was not far from the truth.

When I heard Valentine was coming over to the Mid-Atlantic I couldn't wait to see him but had to work at the Big Bear grocery store during his first booking in Greensboro. We had a young checkout girl and somebody told me she had gone that night. When she stopped by the bottle room to talk I asked her, "Did you see Johnny Valentine?"

"Yes I did! And that man is the devil!" I started joking around with her but she would not change her mind. She was totally scared of Johnny Valentine. He was in the middle of the card that night and he was in the main event from then on. I knew from that moment on, I would never miss a Valentine match.

And I didn't.

Johnny Valentine was around six-two and about two-fifty. His body was always tanned, he looked chiseled in stone and always wore a black robe with crimson lining. One wrestler everybody feared and respected.

Valentine started a gimmick with one thousand silver dollars in a fish bowl as a reward for anyone who could defeat him in ten minutes. It was a brilliant idea that made all his appearances seem more important, Valentine would methodically run his hands through the sliver dollars to help kill time during his matches.

But when he got into the ring he would crush people physically with his slow methodical style. Valentine would slowly stalk his opponents before grabbing them, pulling them over the ropes, then delivering the most punishing forearm smash in wrestling history.

One television match Valentine was tagging with Ric Flair vs Johnny Weaver and a big young kid named Tony Atlas White. White was a body builder from Virginia and Valentine couldn't wait to teach him a lesson. Valentine bent White over the top rope and delivered the Hammering forearm knocking the air out of the youngster with one blow. White immediately fell to his knees trying to regain his breath. Valentine grabbed him up and did it again. This was totally a legal move. Simple but devastating, White was pinned soon after.

I would have paid big money to see him do that to the Road Warriors.

There was another night where Valentine's next TV opponent surprised him—Tim Woods who was a big name under the mask as Mister Wrestling #1. It was a very smartly designed match up.

Valentine sold everything Tim Woods did during that match. He even took a monkey flip out of the turnbuckle which made you believe this Woods guy was the real deal and Valentine was just a bully who was picking on a bunch of jobbers.

It worked. As the crowd cheered for Woods, Valentine bent him over the ropes to deliver the Hammer. All bets were off now. Valentine jerked Woods upward then fell on his leg with an odd twisting motion to break Tim Woods leg. Woods was lying towards the far turnbuckle screaming for help. Valentine stood like a wolf over his prey. Valentine was amazing with his body language. He looked hungry and proud, sending out a brutal message to everyone not to mess with him.

Then he did his interview telling the audience this is what you will get if you try to embarrass him in the future. Valentine was yelling during this interview, not his normal composed self. Johnny even blamed Crockett for bringing in a ringer and trying to embarrass him on television, it worked to perfection.

That was wrestling booking at its finest, Valentine made it work because he was so legit.

Johnny Valentine always took his time in the ring. He was never in a hurry at anything he did. Harley Race was cut from the same piece of cloth. Race and Valentine had two marathon matches in Greensboro that both went fifty plus minutes. Valentine won the US Title here, a first for Greensboro. He won it on two counts. It was the first time the US strap changed hands in Greensboro and the first time Johnny Valentine was cheered.

Race was brought in as Handsome Harley Race from Florida. Those two were arguably the toughest duo in the world at that time and the matches were like two powerful old bulls knocking the crap out of each other. Harley Race brought out the best in Valentine every time they tangled. This title change marked a changing of power in the NWA. The Crockett's became real power players in the NWA, all the big time stars traveled to Greensboro, Charlotte, and Raleigh after that match.

The next big Valentine matches were against Dusty Rhodes and those matches were brilliant in that they were the set ups towards the most re-membered feud in the 1970s, Johnny Valentine vs Wahoo McDaniel.

Rhodes came into Greensboro just before his American Dream run and challenged Johnny. The first match was very odd because Dusty kicked the hell out of Valentine. The match was stopped on a count out with Valentine keeping the title. As Valentine was being helped out of the Coliseum by the referee Dusty jumped off the ring apron and hit him in the back of his head, knocking him four rows into the crowd.

Nobody had ever done that before, a re-match was signed for next month. It was a near sell out. Dusty Rhodes got three and a half minutes of of-fense before Valentine pummeled him for twenty-five. This match was an assassination with Rhodes as the victim and Valentine playing the Angel of Death. Dusty was bleeding from his head and arm while Johnny Valentine took sadistic glee in not even attempting a pin. The referee was begging Valentine to pin him but he only shook his head no. He wanted to keep punishing Rhodes for the last match embarrassment; the crowd went from being entertained and amazed to fearing for Rhodes' well being.

Valentine then climbed to the second rope and dropped an elbow on Rhodes' head, a move Valentine had never attempted before in Greensboro. I counted at least fifteen straight elbow smashes to Dusty Rhodes that night. Back then, Valentine would have pinned his opponent with just one. He began to do these falling fist punches right into Rhodes' arm until blood covered them both. After that, Valentine bit Dusty and the crimson really flowed. With serious life and death overtones the crowd began to yell for the match to be stopped.

There was then a ref bump so no one was left that could stop the carnage. Valentine kept pounding Rhodes, who was by now a bloody mess and incapable of fighting back. Suddenly, Tiger Conway did a run in wearing his street clothes. Valentine saw him coming, he dropped a forearm smash on him and Tiger fell from the ring apron in a heap. Valentine slowly walked over to Rhodes and dropped another elbow on him for good measure. From the back Wahoo McDaniel came running to assist Rhodes. Wahoo was wearing brown slacks, no shirt, and loafers. Valentine grabbed him and ran him down into the ring, post juicing him. Wahoo began to trade chops with Valentine on the ring apron.

Then the drama really began.

From backstage came the Minnesota Wrecking Crew, Ole and Gene Anderson. They began to attack Wahoo. As they trashed Wahoo, Ole instructed Valentine to continue beating Rhodes. And he did. After a couple of minutes all of the wrestlers on the card ran down to stop the match. Ole, Gene and Valentine fought everyone all across the ring with Dusty being dragged around by Valentine, a smear of blood spreading across the ring. It looked like a Spielberg effect but added to the dire urgency to end this match.

The Wrecking Crew were reaching out, grabbing a wrestler and punching him in the face as Valentine continued to drag the fallen Rhodes around the ring. As a group Ole, Gene and Johnny leaped out of the ring right into an erupting crowd of cops and fans. Drinks and punches were thrown both ways. Fans began taking swings with wrestlers and police officers slugging right back. The grapplers had to brawl their way back to the dressing room in a hail of sodas, popcorn, and clenched fists.

It was genius.

I ran over to ringside where the EMTs asked me if it was time for them to enter the fray and assist Dusty. I guess because I'm so tall and looked like I knew what was going on. I told them to wait. Soon a Crockett employee waved them into ring for the Rhodes stretcher job.

Man, he was a mess.

Out of that came the Wahoo / Valentine feud, no one that witnessed a match between these two every forgot it. Every night they put on a physical display of personal destruction that defied description—and sanity. Years later I got to talk with Wahoo and gave him a choice of any wrestling poster from my collection he might want. He chose one with Jack Brisco and Johnny Valentine. "I'll take Valentine! He is the one guy who everyone asks about."

He was really pleased to get that poster so he was very candid with me about the feud. Starting out down in Texas Wahoo's first big feud was against Valentine. Wahoo figured Valentine hated his professional football background and wanted to prove to him that this was a tough business. So he mercilessly crushed him every night. Wahoo said that he fought for his life that first night and it never seemed to get any easier. He soon left for the Carolinas. "And, damn it, Valentine soon followed!"

I said that there was no way any two guys could hit each other any harder than they did and what was the story?

Wahoo told me, "Hell, I don't know. One night I hit him so hard I thought that I knocked his head off and he just stood there. I swear he had chilly bumps on his arm and I think he liked it. He really got off on the contact. I can't begin to explain it. It just was."

Then came the famous plane crash and the Champ never wrestled again. For wrestling fans of the mighty Mid- Atlantic it was never quite the same.

Johnny's son Greg tried to replace his father but was like cardboard in comparison. Greg sold for his opponents and that made him look weak. Johnny Valentine's persona was to always stand strong and deliver an enduring, extreme punishment.

Three Rocks

There were three rocks that never missed a show.

First was Obin Johnson. I met Obin waiting for tickets at the Greensboro Coliseum. Matter of fact, that is where I first met Big Eddie. At every wrestling show I ever went to in the eighties they both were there. It did not matter if it was at a cow barn, those two guys would always be at the show. Hey, wrestling fans like that had to be pitied or admired so we became fast friends.

The Front Row with Bobby & Jackie Fulton.

My favorite Obin moment? There was a Managers Battle Royal once, a total piece of crap. Those matches had to be punishment for poor behavior or a sick rib. There is no reason for a bunch of washed up old fat wrestlers to be in the ring and even think that it could be entertaining. Well, Obin thought it was funny. He almost fell off his chair laughing at these guys. Sir Oliver Humperdink was in the ring and, for some reason, he bladed and started gushing blood all over the place. Obin must have felt that was humorous spot because he started yelling at the top of his lungs, in a high shrill voice, "Juice Humpy Juice!"

I will hear that in my nightmares forever.

Big Eddie Beason was only 15 when he joined the Front Row and you would never have guessed his age. The guy was huge and quiet and loved his grapplers. One night in Winston Salem the Road Warriors jumped out of the ring and humiliated a New Jersey redneck. Hawk went into the crowd wanting a piece of this guy and it could have easily been me he came after. At the next show I mentioned that I was a little afraid of the Roadies because they had more money than me and could afford better lawyers

OBIN   EDDIE   BUD

if they snapped and killed my ass. Big Eddie just looked at me and said, "John, I would not let that happen."

See why I love the big guy? He would have stood in front of the Road Warriors for me!

And last is Bud Grondy—who found his wife on the Front Row and they now have two children and a mortgage to show for it. Bud and I would go anywhere to see a show, he is one of the most decent persons I ever met. My favorite Bud memory was about his weakness, he was one of the biggest Road Warrior marks in the world. At one of the Starrcade shows he failed to notice the Road Warriors had thrown Tully Blanchard and Arn Anderson over the ropes for a DQ, all the Front Row razzed the hell out of Bud. A true vet of the Front Row would have seen that Dusty finish coming from miles away.

So there you have it, three rocks that made wrestling worthwhile. And three of the best friends anyone could ask for.

The Nature Boy

There are great pleasures in my life—friends, family, my comic book and art collection, and watching wrestling for the last half century.

That's right folks, I have been watching wrestling live and on television for forever. I have seen every major pay-for-view in this country and I am not blind yet. Even though now-a-days I wonder why not...

I have seen every major wrestler during that span and Ric Flair was the greatest. Only Terry Funk can be mentioned in the same sentence. And that is the goddamn truth.

I remember watching Flair's first match on TV when he tag teamed with Rip Hawk to destroy a couple of jobbers. Back then if you dropped an elbow on an opponent that was the finish of the match. This new fat kid with a bad blond dye job dropped about five on this one guy—and yelled "Whoooo!" every time he did it.

The television announcer, Charlie Harville, exclaimed that this kid Flair was a sadist who loved punishing his opponents.

After the match came a ringside interview where Rip Hawk did all the talking, introducing this new guy Ric Flair as his cousin. With no warning Flair jumped in front of the microphone and started yelling that, with Uncle Rip's guidance, his future would be bright and then let loose with another "Whoooo!"

Who was this guy? Well, he became the greatest of them all.

Flair learned a lot in a very short time at the side of Johnny Valentine. I remember an interview where Flair asked Johnny the Champ to teach him a great finishing hold and asked if he could get him a date with Joey Heatherton! (I am I dating my self or what?) The finisher was the Brain Buster suplex, a move that Flair used long before the figure-four leg lock.

Then came the plane crash.

The crash was front page news in the Mid Atlantic Territory, it took place in Wilmington, NC just short of the airport. Tim Woods, Ric Flair, David

Crockett, Bob Bruggers and Johnny Valentine were all on board. Bruggers, an ex-football player never wrestled after the crash. Tim Woods was a good guy but he was riding with a bunch of Heels so they changed the report to read Tim Woodin as a passenger, Woods real name. Woods returned to wrestle and so did Flair, of course. David Crockett went on to become a shill babyface announcer.

The pilot died a month later from his injuries. Johnny Valentine was sitting next to the pilot and had his back broken. He never walked again. I always hoped that he would make a comeback because he was so damn tough. He never did. Sadly, he died twenty years later, broke living in Texas.

Crockett quickly brought in Greg Valentine to replace Johnny; he was billed as Johnny's brother but he was really his son. Greg became a huge deal in the Mid-Atlantic, soon taging with Flair. (Greg still wrestles to this day in the small world of the independents.)

I often think that wrestling history would have changed if Johnny Valentine had returned to wrestling, he probably would have won the World Title before Flair.

I did send Flair and Valentine a homemade get well card that weekend and to this day I vividly recall Flair's first return interview where he kept Joey Heatherton and Rachel Welch's card and tore mine to shreds.

After his return, Flair jumped to the top of the wrestling world during a classic feud with Wahoo McDaniel. People still talk about that hard-hitting feud. Anyone in the building could hear those chops and I am sure they are still echoing somewhere in conversation today.

The Feud of the Seventies started when Flair ripped a leg off of a ringside table and hit Wahoo in the head for the finish of a match. Wahoo received multiple stitches that night and Flair called the hospital repeatedly to check on the Chief.

Another great feud of that time happened when, in an interview, Flair told Blackjack Mulligan it was time for him to retire because the big cowboy was "washed up."

That face-off was a classic, Flair ran and bumped forever for Blackjack that night; it was one of those images one can never forget when Flair suplexed Blackjack. Like Atlas holding up the earth, it was very similar to what Kurt

Angle looks like holding the Big Show today. No special effects folks, Flair just jacked up Blackjack's 320 pounds and held him up in the air for as long as he cared to.

I was in attendance the night that Flair and a young punk named Greg Valentine took on the Anderson Brothers for the World Tag Title. I knew the Andersons, at that time, were the toughest bastards in the world and would shut these young punks up.

Fans didn't buy into Greg as a tough guy because they had witnessed his father Jommy not selling for anyone. Greg sold a lot for his opponents and it made him look like a pussy in comparison. This was billed as the family feud and it turned out to be a changing of the guard with Flair and Valentine sending Gene Anderson to the hospital and winning the title.

Then along came Ricky Steamboat and the whole wrestling world took notice. Here were two guys in their prime blowing everyone away with their athletic bumping. And Flair had the perfect guy to play off of. The straight handsome, good guy and the playboy jet set bad boy.

It was the feud that all will be measured against forever.

It's very hard to properly explain why these two clicked so well but I always felt it was that, instead of two middle aged pot-bellied wrestlers, we were instead given two young vibrant guys. And Flair continued wrestling for another 20 years. Amazing.

Ric Flair is a real live superhero.

MID-ATLANTIC CHAMPIONSHIP

WRESTLING — **WAR MEMORIAL COLISEUM**
GREENSBORO
SUN. NOV. 9 7:15 P. M.

17 BIG MATCHES

U.S. CHAMPIONSHIP TOURNAMENT

WITH NAMES SUCH AS

RED BASTION	RAY STEVENS
DUSTY RHODES	TERRY FUNK
RUFUS R. JONES	GENE ANDERSON
OLE ANDERSON	STEVE STRONG
SUPER STAR BILLY GRAHAM	
KEN PATERA	BLACKJACK MULLIGAN
PAUL JONES	WAHOO McDANIEL
TIM WOODS	PROFESSOR MALENKO
HARLEY RACE	TIGER CONWAY, JR.

The True Mid-Atlantic Title Story

At the Greensboro Coliseum to pick up the Front Row's seats I glanced at a listing of the matches, the first of which was an eye opener for old time fans. Black Bart versus Sam Houston who, at one time, had a big feud going for the Mid-Atlantic Title. I'll bet those guys fought for six to eight months for the strap and now, alas, it had come down to this, a curtain jerker.

My how times change. And how people forget. Forget? Not the Front Row!

Those two guys must have fallen on hard times, they both had to work but to fall that far down the chain was kind of shocking. Please don't misunderstand, these two guys weren't exactly in a league with Bobby Eaton but they shouldn't be forgotten. So I went to work on one of the goofiest stunts I ever attempted at a rasslin card.

I made a fake Mid-Atlantic Belt. I got my hands on some cardboard and drew up the belt from memory. I filled in the Crockett logo and on the side panels wrote Sam Houston on one side and Black Bart on the other. Sam was saying, "Hi yall!" And Bart said, "Dag gum it!" It was the feud that would not die.

Some magic markers and staples and it was done. It was one ugly stroke of genius but everybody on the Front Row thought I was nuts.

The big day finally arrived and there I was with this work of art searching for the announcer Tony Gillum to properly announce that this match was for the title. Tony for some reason (job security) refused.

That never stopped me before but as the wrestlers came to the ring a problem came up. Black Bart was a no show! I should have guessed that, it said on my ticket, "all the matches were subject to change." Substituting for Bart was the legendary jobber, Joe Cruz.

It was too late to change the belt so it had to do. We all begged Tony Gillum again to announce that the match but as I said, he would not do it. So

I did it.

I am a loud mouth so I stood up and proudly announced that this match was for the vacant Mid-Atlantic Title! The crowd really got a laugh out of that and the match got underway.

Sam Houston walked over to me and said he was going to win the belt. The wrestlers took to the idea, I guess out of boredom. Joe Cruz started the match on the offensive and put Houston in a front face lock. As he looked at us, Cruz looked at me and said he was going to win the title. I looked at him and said, "Considering the fact that you have never won a match, I doubt it. But if a miracle does happen and you do win this match, the title will be held up by the commissioner. Me."

Both guys lost it laughing.

Just as we figured the match would go, Sam Houston won with a bulldog. As Houston was announced the winner he jumped out of the ring and ran over to us and hugged both Bruce Mitchell and I saying, "Thanks for remembering!" Sam Houston grabbed the belt and carried it over his head back to the dressing room a happy champion.

I have often wondered what the reaction was to Houston bringing that thing back for all to see. A bittersweet moment because Sam really stunk after his match.

A year later, I saw Houston in a match and I yelled where was his Mid-Atlantic Belt? He laughed and said his wife only lets him wear it around the house.

Ladies and gentlemen, that is truly a paper champion at its finest.

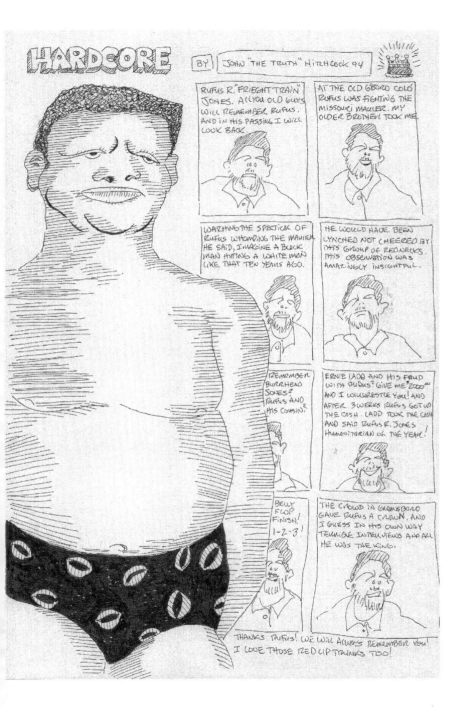

HARDCORE

BY JOHN "THE TRUTH" HITCHCOCK 94

RUFUS R. "FRIEGHT TRAIN" JONES. ALL YOU OLD GUYS WILL REMEMBER RUFUS. AND IN HIS PASSING I WILL LOOK BACK.

AT THE OLD GBORO COLO RUFUS WAS FIGHTING THE MISSOURI MAULER. MY OLDER BROTHER TOOK ME.

WATCHING THE SPETICAL OF RUFUS WHOMPING THE MAULER HE SAID, IMAGINE A BLACK MAN HITTING A WHITE MAN LIKE THAT TEN YEARS AGO.

HE WOULD HAVE BEEN LYNCHED NOT CHEERED BY THIS GROUP OF REDNECKS. THIS OBSERVATION WAS AMAZINGLY INSIGHTFUL.

REMEMBER BURRHEAD JONES? RUFUS AND HIS COUSIN?

ERNIE LADD AND HIS FEUD WITH RUFUS? GIVE ME \$2000° AND I WILL WRESTLE YOU! AND AFTER 3 WEEKS RUFUS GOT UP THE CASH. LADD TOOK THE CASH AND SAID RUFUS R. JONES HUMANITARIAN OF THE YEAH!

BELLY FLOP FINISH! 1-2-3!

THE CROWD IN GREENSBORO GAVE RUFUS A CROWN, AND I GUESS IN HIS OWN WAY TERRIBLE INTERVIEWS AND ALL HE WAS THE KING.

THANKS RUFUS! WE WILL ALWAYS REMEMBER YOU! I LOVE THOSE RED CUP TRUNKS TOO!

109

The Weightlifting Challenge

We have one of those Lets Start Up A Feud spectaculars that the fine folks at Crockett Promotions were famous for.

The good old coliseum crowd of lets say 12,000 plus had taken the bait, we all settled in for the Classic Weight Lifting Challenge between The Legion of Doom, the Road Warriors along with Paul Ellering versus The Powers of Pain with its team of the Barbarian and Warlord with Number One Paul Jones.

I always call Paul Jones "Number One" because that was his old moniker during his face days, whenever Jones would pass by the Front Row I would yell that at him. Being Number One he would always slyly put out his index finger as he passed by. He never forgot his fans.

Everyone in Greensboro knew the Challenge was going to be an angle to focus heat on The Powers of Pain; boy did they need it. I personally liked The Barbarian because he would kick the shit out of whoever he was facing.

And I do mean kick. That was his big finishing move—lift his foot over his head and kick wrestlers right in the mouth My favorite boot shot other than a Bruiser Brody was in Florida when The Barbarian in an outside the ring brawl turned and delivered a boot shot in the face of one Scott Hall and basically knocked his teeth out. Big Scott Hall was doing a run in and took the boot full force and just staggered away. Did he really knock out his teeth? I thought so and that is a reality, isn't it?

The Warlord was, and I'm sure still is, a huge juice guy that really sucked. He looked good with a bald head and bushy goatee but that was it. He was kind of like Hulk Hogan with no superman comeback.

The Road Warriors were a big deal. Everyone in attendance couldn't wait to see how much these guys could lift. It wasn't wrestling it was showbiz.

Needless to say the Front Row cheered for the Heels so it was just a guess as to when the Heel Turn would happen.

We knew it would. It always did.

It was a constant of great Pro Wrestling. Everyone but Bud that is. Bud Grondy was thrilled to see his heroes up close and cheered like a fourteen year old girl for the Road Warriors.

(I was never so embarrassed in my life.)

Anyway, the crowd was really hot for this angle and cheered the set up. There was a bench press, a ton of weights and a box of chalk. See, a great set up takes little effort. The Warriors must have had a plane to catch because after one lift they wanted the weight raised to 600lbs. The crowd went nuts and Bud jumped up and down with glee.

Remember when I said I was never so embarrassed? Change that.

Now that I think about it, Ivan Koloff was there in support of the Powers of Pain. Remember: Heel Rule Number One, if Ivan Koloff is evolved in an angle it is going to turn out really bad for the faces. You can never trust a Commie Rat! But in our case we just loved the guy.

John, Ivan, and Obin.

As Animal got on the bench press to lift the great weight, Number One Paul Jones hit Animal with the box of chalk and the Heels beat the hell out of the immortal Road Warriors. Man oh man! We all popped big for that. Animal was trapped under the 600-pound bar as the Barbarian and Warlord kicked and hit him. Hawk was tossed into the weights leaving him out of the action.

Then the Heels ran away.

The Crocketts really wanted to sell this angle so out came the stretcher. This was the first Stretcher Job that the Roadies ever did in the Mid-Atlantic so the fans really bought it as real. The referees carefully put Animal on the stretcher and wheeled him out of the Coliseum. Only one problem. The referees got mixed up and were moving Animal the wrong way! They forgot the directions to the dressing room. I guess that Animal's injuries were not as life threatening as we all thought.

Slowly they pushed the injured athlete directly past the Front Row. I was thinking that maybe I should throw myself screaming on Animal for effect but as they got closer I chickened out. Are those guy huge or what? I think Bruce gave them all the Four Horsemen four fingers and Bud started to cry.

Well, he should have.

As we were leaving the arena a few skeptical fans knocked over the weights to see if they were legit. David Crockett got pissed at that even though it really made the angle by doing so. Come to think of it when wasn't David Crockett pissed about something?

MID-ATLANTIC CHAMPIONSHIP

WRESTLING

WAR MEMORIAL COLISEUM

GREENSBORO

SAT. JAN. 31

8:15 P. M.

TRIPLE MAIN EVENT

MID-ATLANTIC TITLE MATCH

RIC FLAIR

Versus

WAHOO McDANIEL

BLACKJACK vs TIM
MULLIGAN   WOODS

U.S. HEAVYWEIGHT TITLE

ANGELO MOSCA vs PAUL JONES

MONGOLS vs TIGER CONWAY & DANNY MILLER

HAYSTACKS CALHOUN   Versus   MIKE DUBOIS

EL RAYO & ROBERTO SOTO vs STEVE STRONG & DOUG GILBERT

RON GARVIN   Versus   LARRY SHARP   *   TIO TIO TIO   Versus   JOE TURNER

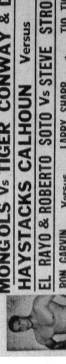

 **HARDCORE** BY

JOHN "GO TARHEELS!" HITCHCOCK 94

TODAY THIS STRIP IS DEALING WITH THE SUBJECT OF DEADWOOD AT **W.C.W.** YOU KNOW WHO YOU ARE.

I HAVE COUNTED 26 PIECES OF DEADWOOD, AND ALLOW ME TO INTRODUCE THEM TO YOU.

ATLANTA GA.

FIRST, HERE IS JOHNNY B. BADD. A PERFECT NAME I MIGHT AD.

BOTH SHOCKMASTERS REGULAR AND UNLEADED. DUSTY IS GONE AND SO ARE YOU CLUMSEY FUCK.

THE FUCKIN TERRIBLE KONGS. OH! NO! JUST WHAT WE NEED ANOTHER FAT GUY!

MAXIMUM PAIN. MAN WHAT A WORTHLESS GUY! PRAY ME A TUNE FATMAN. SOMEBODY BREAK HIS HAND!

RICK RUDE. HEY! DO NOT ACT SURPRISED! HE SUCKS HARD AND LOUD. THE WINNER OF THE Jimmy GARVIN AWARD OF COZY.

STOP THE MUSIC.

THE "USELESS, NO ONE WOULD BUY A TICKET TO SEE" COLE TWINS.

DUH? DUH?

THUNDER AND LIGHTING. MAN! WHO DO THESE GUYS BLOW? JIM BARRNETT MAYBE?

I WOULD ONLY SPARE DUSTIN IF HE WOULD TURN HEEL AND SLOP IS OLD FAT FATHER. NOW THAT'S GREAT T.V.

SLAP!

TAKE THAT FAT MAN!

THE "I DO THE SAME MATCH EVERY DAY OF OUR LIVES" NASTY BOYS! HEY CHANGE THEIR NAMES TO THE FAT BOYS OK!

ZZZ!

ZZZZZZZ

THE QUEEN OF DEADWOOD MISSY. (HEY! SHE GIVES ME A WOODY.) THE ONLY PERSON WHO LIKES HER IS MANK "I HATE HER UNTIL SHE TALKS TO ME" MADDAN.

ICE TRAIN AND RON SIMMONS. I WOULD CAN THEM JUST FOR THAT FUED THAT LASTED 1½ MONTHS FOR ZERO DOLLARS.

FSU

COL. ROB PARKER. CAN YOU SAY, SUCKS! GO BACK TO HOCKEY YOU USELESS ASSHOLE.

DO I HEAR PAUL JONES CALLING HIM BACK?

ERIC WATTS. HEY DUDE DADDY'S GONE, AND SO ARE YOU. ROOKIE OF THE YEAR MY ASS!

LOOKS A LITTLE LIKE KENDAL WINDUM

AND THE ASSASSIN, CHRIS CHAMPION, AND TEX AND SHANGHI. HIT THE ROAD JACK AND DON'T YA COME BACK NO MORE, NO MORE NO MORE!

BURN! BABY! BURN!

HEY I FORGOT JUNGLE JIM! HARLEM HEAT! , TEDDY LONG, TODD "CLUMSEY FUCK" CHAMPION!

114

MID-ATLANTIC CHAMPIONSHIP

WRESTLING

GREENSBORO COLISEUM

GREENSBORO, N. C.

SUN. MAY 28 7:30 P.M.

WORLD TAG TEAM TITLE MATCH

GREG VALENTINE & RIC FLAIR

Versus

RICKY STEAMBOAT

And

PAUL JONES

MID-ATLANTIC TITLE MATCH

KEN PATERA CHAMPION Vs SENSATIONAL **DICK MURDOCK**

TONY ATLAS And Versus **RUFUS R. JONES**

BARON VON RASCHKE And **CYCLONE NEGRO** Versus **MR. WRESTLING**

GENE ANDERSON Versus **SGT. JACQUES GOULET**

ROBERTO SOTO Versus

MR. SATO Vs MR. X 1 ★ ★ ★ ★ SKANDOR AKBAR Vs JERRY STUBBS

Top of the World Ma!

Another spectacular at the Greensboro Coliseum, the main event—Nature Boy Ric Flair versus Jimmy Garvin locked inside a steel cage. Flair had to put up the World Title up against Garvin's wife Precious for one night of monkey love. The stakes were high and this was the big blow off for that feud.

Of course the Coliseum was packed and we all were in our customary Front Row seats awaiting the action. The ring crew came out for the main event and began to assemble the cage. Legendary Mid- Atlantic jobber Klondike Bill for some odd reason sat down on the floor right in front of me. This opportunity was too good a chance to pass up so I started a conversation with Klondike Bill.

One of the smartest things I ever did.

The guy was a riot with a great sense of humor. I leaned over and asked Bill if the Heels were going to run out and kick his ass tonight and get the keys to the cage?

Bill replied—and I quote—"Why? Did you hear something?" I just about fell off my chair laughing at that one. Bill told me, "You know, I never understood why they just don't come out and ask me for the key, after all I would rather just give it to them."

The night got better and better with us peppering Bill with questions. He told us we should have seen the Orange Bowl when they dropped the cage the night of the first War Games. "That was something!" He was very proud of the accomplishment from a technical standpoint.

Well, out to the ring strutted JJ Dillon with his arm in a sling, David

Crockett and Doctor Tom Miller sat ringside. Then Garvin, Precious, and Flair entered the ring.

The crowd was fire hot. Any match with Flair in it was exciting and he was really getting Garvin over. The match was about 15 minutes in when Flair put Garvin in the Figure Four Leg Lock. They were both in the corner nearest to us when all hell broke loose. Precious was screaming for help when this crazy fan exploded out of the crowd and began climbing up the cage!

Who said valor is dead?

And this guy was really scurrying up the cage quickly. JJ Dillon tried to grab the person's foot but with his arm in a sling he really couldn't do much. David Crockett attempted to stop the guy but the nut was really fired up and kicked Crockett. It was a really beautiful shot right in Crockett's big mouth, something that all fans listening to his pussy whining for years would have been proud of. This crazed fan made it all the way to the top of the cage then suddenly froze. He had nowhere to go but down and it was a long way down.

Flair and Garvin both witnessed what was happening and were freaking out. Flair looked up and yelled, "God Damn!"

I figured that it was time to nudge Klondike Bill. "Hey Klondike."

"Yeah?"

"See that guy on top of the cage?"

"Yeah."

"He is not part of the show."

"Really? I guess I better get him down then."

Bill casually walked over, grabbed the kook by his leg and ripped him off the cage. Cops showed up and dragged him away. Bill came back and said, "You know, I should have let him get in there. Then we would have had something really worth seeing."

While Klondike was ripping this nut down Garvin was submitting to Flair, trapped in the Figure Four. What could they do? That intruder looked like he was about to fall on top of them at any moment. David Crockett turned to us and said, "Nobody fucks up my show!"

Like he did anything.

.

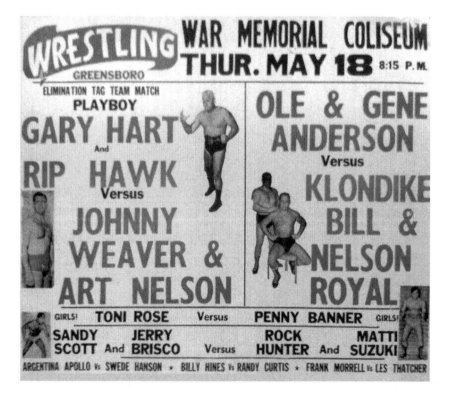

MID-ATLANTIC CHAMPIONSHIP

WRESTLING

GREENSBORO COLISEUM
GREENSBORO, N. C.

SAT. OCT. 8
8:30 P. M.

TRIPLE MAIN EVENT

U.S. TITLE MATCH

RIC FLAIR
Versus
RICKY STEAMBOAT

FALLS COUNT ANYWHERE

MASKED SUPER STAR
Versus
PAUL JONES

MR. WRESTLING
Versus
BARON VON RASCHKE

RUSSIAN STOMPER Versus **TIGER CONWAY**

MR. X I And **MR. X II** Vs **TED OATES** And **TULLY BLANCHARD**

HARTFORD LOVE vs **MR. SATO** ★ **ROBERTO SOTO** vs **RICK FERARA** ★ **FRANK MONTE** vs **DANNY MILLER**

Double A

My favorite wrestler of all time is Arn Anderson. No doubt about it.

Arn wasn't the best wrestler and sadly I doubt that he will be in any hall of fame but he should be. When I think of Arn I feel I should just turn a tap on the side of my head and let all the stories just flow out on this page but I would be laughing too hard to type all those wonderful moments. But, here goes.

The first interview I ever remember by Arn was when he said he wasn't the kind of guy to blow his own horn but... "TOOT! TOOT!"

There was an amazing confidence that just exploded on the television and talk about charisma—well, Arn had that in buckets. This was during the Crockett Mid-Atlantic TV period and Arn soon became the guy to watch and listen too.

He never had a boring match or interview and all my friends loved it when he was hand picked by Ole Anderson to be his partner in the new Minnesota Wrecking Crew. Funny, usually the new guy would shut up and do all the wrestling but that was not Arn. He did the bulk of the wrestling during the match and would steal the interview with one or two lines. And Ole Anderson was a great interview and maybe considered the best talker of the late '80s. Arn having such a powerful presence and standing out so quickly was no easy feat. He just acted like he belonged.

And he had this uncanny body language that told you a lot about how he felt about someone. Few ever mastered that extra touch but Arn did. His interview skills were very simple but very effective. He basically beat a guy mercilessly with the truth. His truth, mind you, but he got his point across like few could.

Arn continued to shine, it was easy to see why he became one of the Horseman. Dusty Rhodes was a very lucky man and knew what he had in guys like Flair, Blanchard, Eaton, Morton and Arn Anderson. These guys could work and sell better than anyone in the business. They seemed to balance out the great Mid-Atlantic Territory.

The secret of great Heels is that they have to be the best workers on the

card to sell all the face's moves. And boy did they.

A strange thing happened. The Horsemen were cheered on by the crowd and the promotion never seemed to understand why. They were portrayed as cool bad guys with chicks on their arms and cash to wave around. Smarter and much more prepared than the faces. When Dusty Rhodes got jumped in a parking lot by the Four Horsemen, he looked like a fool with no friends. And how can you cheer for a fool?

Arn was no fool.

Another strange thing happened. The more fans cheered the Horsemen the more people understood just how badly Dusty sucked as a wrestler. A landslide started when the ego-driven Rhodes got booed all the time and the Heels began to be cheered.

The Horsemen did house interviews talking about their fans in Greensboro. This put a lot of heat on us but we would cheer like hell and create signs to show our support. Back then nobody made signs, man did we stand out. Every week there would be an Arn or Tully interview about something we did at a match, what a sign said and what was going to happen at the next show. It was heaven.

One time I made scorecards and we all began to rate the moves and matches. It was a simple thing but it went thought the roof locally. The channel 12 late news did a feature on the rating system in wrestling and showed us giving the moves and matches a score. "That is what the world needs to help us learn what is good wrestling and bad wrestling," the news anchor added, tongue in cheek.

Arn did an interview saying he liked the scorecards so naturally the Horsemen got tens across the board. That night he was going to wrestle the Junkyard Dog and we would need fractions to keep score.

The greatest tag team match I ever saw was Tully and Arn battling The Midnight Express, Bobby Eaton and Stan Lane. JJ Dillon was positioned in one corner with the Horsemen and Jim Cornette in the other. It was a night of magic, those six professionals put on an exhibition of timing and match flow that few have equaled. I sat astonished by the command they had over the crowd and each other.

The audience didn't have a favorite, they just cheered each move and counter play, really getting into the excitement. One of the fantastic underpinnings of live grappling is the set up where a wrestler will repeat a series of moves so you begin to anticipate the next move. Then they do a variation or change it up, which startles the viewer. These change-ups were going on throughout the entire match, blowing everyone away. Big reason why I loved wrestling during that period.

Later on Arn and Tully left for the WWF and the gap in talent was huge. They were one of the best tag teams in the world, did we all miss them. The Horsemen imploded until Flair and Arn returned to WCW a year later. Tully did not return however, he was being screwed and squeezed on his contract. Arn and Tully never got back together, as a result a lot of the magic was gone. They seemed to think alike, the blueprint of tag team wrestling for my money.

When Arn returned to Greensboro he wrestled Bob Cook and our signs were everywhere welcoming Arn back home. He threw Cook out of the ring and made him read the Welcome Home Arn sign we made. As Arn stood in the ring he turned, looked at us and said, "Man, It's great to be

home!" I still have the TV taping in Greensboro and it is an amazing thing to watch.

Arn once said in an interview that Greensboro was Home Court for the Horsemen. To me that meant the Heels were never going to lose a match in the Coliseum—and they rarely did. We got away with murder from then on out because we could talk all the trash we wanted and the Heels would back it up with a win.

I got the crazy idea to make life sized Arn Anderson masks for the whole Front Row to wear during his match. We had a sign that read, "Arn Nation." He loved it and the fans began asking for Arn Anderson Masks. I swear I could have sold them.

Later a friend came by the store I worked for and showed me his Christmas gift. It was an Arn Mask made into a lamp. It was the stupidest, funniest thing I have ever seen but Arn was the man. I wish I had one now.

We carpooled up to Asheville one day for a WCW Pay Per View that featured Arn versus Ric Flair. That was another classic, something I never thought I would ever see but WCW didn't understand how important this match was and cut the time short. Pillman did a Run In for the finish.

It was an incredible match as Arn held his own with the legend, his best friend Flair.

Oddly, Arn returned to the ring in Winston Salem for the first match after the near fatal fight with Sid. Arn walked around to our side of the ring and shook everyone's hand. His face was marked and his body had small cuts and short brown slashes. I told him it was great to have him back, we were worried about him. We would have had a sign but we didn't know he was on the card that night. He thanked us and assured everyone he was okay.

Arn had to retire from wrestling due to a neck and back injury. The night in, night out pounding had taken its toll and he never performed again. WCW did let Arn have his farewell on television, it was an amazing moment when he started to cry and retired for real.
Behind him were Chris Benoit and Flair who were both crying as well.

It was a chilling moment but, of course, WCW let this great honest moment be put up for sport the following week by the N.W.O. They should all be ashamed for making fun of a man's career like that. And the fact that he could never really fight back at Hall, Nash, or Xpac for doing it made it suck even worse.

The bastards.

A week or two later I went backstage to present Arn with a framed cartoon of the Front Row holding up signs saying, "Arn 4 Ever!" Arn told me he was going to put it up in his den.

Thanks Arn, you are the greatest. Always will be.

ARN ANDERSON

Flair Stories

There are two stories I need to tell about the Nature Boy.

Flair and I are not pals that hang out and swap stories. When fans from out of state show up they think that, since I am from Greensboro, the hotbed of the Mid-Atlantic, that we all partied with the wrestlers after every show. That's just not true. Those talented wrestlers usually packed up and went on to the next show in Charlotte and did not stay here in town so we rarely ever met our heroes.

Well one time Bruce got word that Flair was going to be at the Four Season bar and he wanted to say hello. At that time Flair had a string of Gold's Gyms opening and one was on Market Street here in Greensboro.

Flair? Bar? Wanted to talk? Shit, I am there.

When Bruce and I got there, well, Flair was already there talking with a nice lady who ran his gym. We walked up and said hello and the Legend asked if we wanted a beer. Now, I do not drink but if Ric Flair is buying me a beer, I am taking one. I swear all I could think about is for the rest of my life I can always say I hung out in a bar and the Ric Flair bought me a beer.

As we were talking two very out of place guys walked into the bar. Out of place was being really nice. These two guys looked like they fell off a turnip truck and awkwardly stood at the back of the bar. Flair saw them and looked at us and said, "Excuse me."

Flair walked over to these two guys and introduced himself. He then answered a few quick questions, signed a few autographs and thanked them for going to the matches and thanked them for stopping by.

I stood there slack jawed and could not believe how kind he was to these two oddballs. And I told Flair I thought that was the coolest thing I have ever seen. Flair looked at me and said flatly that was a part of his job.

If you really think about it, Flair was a hot heel for years so those two guys could have wanted to settle a feud for something he did to Wahoo ten years ago. That was an example of just how classy Ric Flair was and still is in my book.

My other Flair story comes a few years later.

My brother Bob got terrific seats on the 40 yard line for the first Carolina Panthers playoff game against the Dallas Cowboys, this was the largest crowd in Panther history and a very tough ticket to get. I was the designated driver since I was sober as a judge while the other guys, Wiles, Simp, and Bob wanted to celebrate the huge game. That is just a nice way of saying they wanted to do some serious drinking. During half time Bob stumbled up to me to say he saw Flair up in the crowd. "Lets go say hello to The Nature Boy!" So we did just that.

Flair was sitting with the families of the team, I guess one of the players hooked him up with the seats. I walked up to where Flair was sitting, up above myself and my brother, and said, "We still love you in Greensboro, Nature Boy."

Flair broke out in a huge smile and asked how was I doing and how were all the guys in Greensboro. Then my little brother went off, "Hey, Nature Boy! You are the kiss stealing, wheeling dealing, son of a gun! How come you got such shitty seats? We are sitting way down there and you are sitting way up here. What is your problem? What is the deal?"

Both Flair and I fell out laughing at that line.

I turned to Flair and told him to enjoy the game and dragged Bob back to our seats. I can't blame Bob for talking shit, that might be the only time I ever had better seats than Ric Flair.

The Panthers won that game, a night to remember. More for Nature Boy than the game.

First Great American Bash

Talk about wasted youth—when the advertising for the Great American Bash first appeared I knew I had to be there. This promised to be quite a trip as it was an outdoor event in Charlotte and it was pouring rain in Greensboro, ninety miles away. That show was a horror to get to but the weather got better as we made it to the football stadium where the event was held.

Not going wasn't an option, bad weather or not, we were lucky to score second row seats and this was going to be a huge show—Flair versus Nikita Koloff with David Crockett as special referee for the main event.

We were forced to park about twelve blocks away on a side street and hoof it to the stadium. As we got closer you could hear the excited crowd popping—the matches had already begun. Imagine that, they didn't hold the start for their biggest fans! When we did finally get to our seats we found ourselves sitting on the grass and in the mud. This was going to be a real strange show.

The Road Warriors were fighting the Russians, Ivan and Crusher and we soon noticed that Road Warrior Hawk had eaten an orange for lunch. How did we know that? He threw it up in the first twenty seconds of the match! Man, that was an ugly sight that kind of made me a little hungry, so I ordered a chili dog.

The Russian / Road Warrior feud was blazing hot, the fans really hated those commies. Heat was on that night, it got really hairy when suddenly fifteen Harley Davidson riding Hells Angels decided they wanted to kill Ivan and Crusher.

I am not kidding. These roughnecks went though the crowd knocking people on their cans as they made their way towards the ring. It was a near riot situation and the Hells Angels started throwing bottles and beer cans at the Russians from ringside. I couldn't believe the hatred these guys had.

Ivan was yelling at David Crockett to get some security up there to stop the madness. Nobody was trying to stop them, fortunately the Hells Angels decided to leave on their own. If they would have made it into the ring— well I might have stood up and kicked some ass but as you folks know by now I am a pussy and sober. Luckily, everything seemed to fall in order. For a short while.

Kamala the Ugandan Giant battled Magnum TA and, thank God, Uganda was not good friends with the USSR. Magnum won with another belly to belly finish that had been demonstrated about a thousand times on television.

At last came the big main event with Flair versus Nikita.

Nikita was in the ring with his uncle Ivan Koloff as Flair arrived at the stadium in a helicopter. What a way to enter a main event, the crowd loved it. Well, some in the crowd did, anyway.

The place was a nuthouse with fans breaking into fistfights all over the stadium. Police would storm into the crowd to use their billy clubs on them and drag the troublemakers out feet first. I can still remember the sound of peoples' heads banging on concrete as Charlotte's finest dragged those folks

down the steps.

Come to think of it... where were those same cops when Ivan and Crusher were almost attacked? Maybe they believed the hype.

The main event was a fantastic match until Ivan started to interfere. Then things got out of hand again. I was sitting on the outside aisle when a frenzied fan bolted for the ring. He tripped over me, I could have lied and said I tried to stop him but he went by in a blur, directly up into the ring to give Ivan a knee in the balls. Ivan doubled over, yelling at David Crockett once again about the lack of security.

The intruder would not back down so Nitkita went after him. He didn't catch him but the cops did and they kicked the living shit out of this guy. It was brutal.

Now you know why I only hit the ring once in my career but that is another story. Flair won the match with the cheap help of Crockett but that was not the action I will remember.

MID-ATLANTIC CHAMPIONSHIP

WRESTLING

GREENSBORO COLISEUM

SUN. JAN. 22 7:30 P.M.

GREENSBORO, N. C.

TRIPLE MAIN EVENT

RETURN TITLE MATCH FOR THE U. S. TITLE

BLACKJACK MULLIGAN

CHAMPION

Versus

RICKY STEAMBOAT

MID-ATLANTIC HEAVYWEIGHT CHAMPIONSHIP MATCH

GREG VALENTINE

CHAMPION

Versus

WAHOO McDANIEL

RIC FLAIR vs PAUL JONES

SIX MAN TAG TEAM MATCH

TIGER CONWAY
BOBO BRAZIL
MIGHTY IGOR

Versus

CRUSHER BLACKWELL
MISSOURI MAULER
CYCLONE NEGRO

HARTFORD LOVE vs MR. SATO ★ CHARLIE FULTON Versus DANNY MILLER ★ RICHARD BLOOD vs BILL WHITE

131

We Have HERD Enough!

I guess it is time to get this one out of the way.

I first started making signs about 30 years ago. My first was a logical choice; it was a sign for Ric Flair. It was on white typing paper and it spelled out R-I-C. That was it; I guess it was the first heel sign ever.

ONE MORE TIME.

I also made about ten Ric Flair Fan Club buttons that we all wore to the shows. They were real ugly pink and made out of typing paper but people did notice. One group of kids walked over, spotted the button on me and went crazy yelling at me.

One of the kids said that he bet I was the only Ric Flair fan in the building. A friend of mine, Johnny Wooding, turned around wearing a button and said, "Isn't everyone?" All the guys that night had a Flair button on. Rusty Gleason, Jeff Steele, Kelly Brame and Robert Cummings all turned around and said, "Where is your button?"

From then on I drew up signs cheering for the heels. I think it was for the attention mostly but it was a lot of fun when the Heels would acknowledge us. Right after the Tully Blanchard, Magnum TA, I QUIT match, I made a sign that read, "TULLY NEVER QUIT!"

Tully and JJ Dillon saw the sign at the beginning of the match, pointed to it and said I was right. That action got me hit with about four full drink cups but it was worth it. Tully never did quit. He did say and I quote, "Aaaaarrrrrgggreaahhh!" But that is not "I quit" in my book.

All this leads us to the 'We Have Herd Enough' sign. Jim Herd was the most ignorant person who ever ran a wrestling company—and that is quite a statement. He was president of WCW with a history of managing Pizza Huts. Herd thought what wrestling needed was star power and odd gimmicks.

The star power was Robocop at ringside to restore order at one match. His other gimmicks were legendary for their lameness. He had a TV match where the loser was electrocuted in an electric chair. Abdullah the Butcher was fried alive for your entertainment! (Thank God he lives and now runs a rib joint in Atlanta.)

Then he introduced the tag team, the Ding Dongs. These poor guys ran around in a circle with bells on their trunks and got beaten match after match. Then Herd introduced a new tag team called the Hunchbacks. This team would be unbeatable because you could not pin their shoulders down. At one point Herd wanted to change Ric Flair's name to Gladiator Ric.

The above incidents and others are what spurred me on make that sign. As hard as it was at this time I still did watch week after week, I felt I had the right to voice my opinion that the product and leadership of this company was in the hands of a madman that really didn't care how stupid this sport became. And I did care.

The usual practice of making signs was we would all get together at my store and throw ideas back and forth. Then I would letter the good ones.

I knew that all the wrestlers would love it, so I used big black block letters and spelled out, "WE HAVE HERD ENOUGH!" No one knew I made the sign. It was my secret. My four year BFA in painting and graphics had come in handy!

The Rock and Roll vs the Midnight Express match was the perfect opportunity to hold it up because it was going to be a great match that all the fans would pay attention to—and Jimmy Cornette would likely laugh his ass off.

When the time came to hold the sign up the Midnights just fell apart laughing and the camera shot was perfect. You could not miss it. I was right in the middle of the Front Row. It was clearly visible to everyone there and at home.

Security Chief Doug Dillinger walked over and asked me not to hold up the sign. I asked him why? He said, "Because if you hold that sign up again, I might lose my job." Man, I could have gotten Doug fired.

I did sneak the sign in during the Flair versus Lex Lugar main event, Doug and David Crockett just sat there and laughed. At intermission a lot of fans stopped me at the hotdog line to tell me that I spelled Herd wrong. Aaahhh, the public is always keeping me in order.

For the first time ever I went to the hotel bar after the show to hopefully visit with the wrestlers and the hardcore fans I met the day before.

Ron Lemuix said that he called a friend in Florida who was watching the pay per view and said the sign was clearly visible and everyone loved it. That was very cool so I went up to the bar wanting to mingle. Out of nowhere Chris Cruise walked up giving me hell for humiliating his boss. Why did I do it he asked? "If you could have seen the pain on his face when that sign went up!"

I told him it was a joke, that I hated the way the promotion was being run. Then some other toady, Dennis Brent, said out loud that someone should kick my ass! I knew that at 6'3 and 250lbs I could kick his weasel ass with little trouble but his friends were a whole different deal. It was getting uncomfortable to be around all of these people lining up to defend their boss so I got out of there soon after.

The Herd sign became a huge point of controversy over fan's rights in the Wrestling Observer letters page. I replied that if you want a positive sign, do a good wrestling show. That would shut me up.

Two or three months later I ran into Tony Shavonie ringside in Greensboro. Tony saw me holding up a sign that night saying, "Gladiator Ric versus Ben Herd." Tony said that I should hold that one up a little higher so it would get on camera. We both started laughing and I told Tony that he knew, with all his years in Greensboro, that I was definitely going to do something.

During that year he was in the WWF Tony watched the show in Titan Towers along with Vince McMahon and his booking committee. Tony told me when that sign went up everyone in the room fell down laughing for about five minutes. Then Vince got real serious and said that the WWF should start making security plans so that this kind of thing could not happen to them. And they started searching fans and confiscating signs after that.

WCW started checking fans at the door as well, they even began making fake signs to promote the people they were pushing. They'd walk out before tapings and ask everyone to hold up their signs for television. When they saw a sign that they did not like they would wade into the crowd and take it and replace it with a Diamond Dallas Page sign or some such. Shit, I would have rather light myself on fire that to hold up a DDP sign.

Years later I was sitting Front Row in Winston Salem for a WCW TV taping when they began confiscating signs from fans. For some reason all of these signs were stacked right at my feet that night and I felt very, very cold

"Folks, it's all true. I was there that night in Greensboro for "We Have HERD Enough" the all time classic sign. It was the toast of the town and talk of the wrestling press for several weeks."
—D. Bourne

On Tour: Baltimore

"Holy Balls!"
—Ole Anderson

The Front Row made a road trip to Baltimore for the big Flair versus Sting match. We all got word that Flair was going to drop the strap and that was going to be something really special to see in person.

Obin, Big Eddie, Bruce, KC and yours truly took two cars and drove off early in the morning. Simp and The Coach were going to meet us there that night.

This match was right after the Herd Sign in Greensboro so I got a lot of attention. Most was totally undeserved but it was fun. The Florida group with Klon, Jeff Bowdren and Dave Flaherty showed up later.

After Simp and The Coach arrived we went to the room to unpack, at the elevator we ran into Ole Anderson. I told him I was sorry to hear about Gene passing, he was gruff but cool. When the elevator doors opened he told us to get on and we all made small talk. Very small talk, the guy still scared the shit out of all of us. It's one of those childhood things, watching him week after week kick the shit out of Wahoo and Ricky Steamboat. I guess that made us all a little hesitant. I am sure you all understand.

Later we went up to Meltzer's room to hang out and there was a knock on Dave's door. Believe it or not, it was WCW security. These two guys looked like they worked for the CIA with flat top haircuts and wearing suits. They wanted to ask Dave two questions.

First, they wanted to know if the guys from Greensboro were there and were they going to have any signs. I told them that we were on tour and on vacation. No signs tonight. That was good with them because Mr. Herd wanted to make sure that there was not going to be any disturbances at this show. I know you folks think you are reading some kind of bad science fiction or I was on some serious drugs at this time but this is all true.

Second question was to inform all the fans that if anyone put his hands on Ole Anderson, Mr. Anderson would fight back in defense.

Dave turned to the room and asked if anyone had attacked Ole? We all played dumb. But I knew who did it. It had to be Simp. When these WCW guys left we all sat amazed that they gave that much thought about a few nutty fans from Greensboro. It was a total waste of time that they should have been spending on booking the show.

A little later I ran into Simp and asked him if he had attacked Ole. Simp told me, "Aaaah, Igor I just saw big ol' Ole and slapped a head lock on him and said, "HEY OLE! YOU BIG BASTARD! LET'S RASSLE!" Needless to say, Simp had a few too many drinks at the bar but I think you probably guessed that by now.

The show was excellent and the Flair /Sting title change electric. The crowd could sense the title change coming, the heat was amazing to experience in person.

We were told the place to eat was a restaurant named Sabatinos at the Inner Harbor so off we went. When we got there it was packed—by sheer luck the wait staff put the Front Row in a room with Sting, Luger, the Steiners and Tom Zenk. During the meal Luger and Sting would look over at our motley crew and start laughing. The finest seafood I have ever eaten, shrimp the size of softballs and the people were very nice to all of us.

After eating we walked over the wrestler's table to say hello. Luger wanted to know why we didn't have any Lex Looser signs? Sting said he always thought that Stink was a nice touch. The Steiner Brothers didn't care if we were there or not. And who really cares what Zenk thought anyway.

I asked Sting about his knee, he told me the whole story. Of course I wanted to know if Doug Dillinger was going to get a title shot since he put him out of action. Later that night Simp passed out in his pizza..

Trip to Florida:
Bruce, Dave Flaherty, myself, and Obin.

On Tour: Florida

Flair versus Fujinami was the main event at St. Petersburg and the Front Row crew jumped on a plane and went down to the Sunshine State. Florida is a hot damn wrestling state and every wrestling newsletter subscriber in the country was there. We all met up with the Florida and Atlanta groups at the hotel. Man, it was great seeing all those guys. I wish they were chicks but you can't have every thing.

There was an independent show not too far away on the day before the big show so everybody took off for rasslin action. The show was outside on a shuffleboard court with a lot of old steel chairs around the ring. The place was wild. Every obsessed fan in the country was there and the Front Row felt pressure to turn this shindig on its head. I looked at Bruce and Obin and we knew it was time to put up or shut up. It was time for Greensboro to show everybody just what the Front Row was all about.

And we did.

I think we yelled at everyone at sight. I yelled at some young rowdy kid that was cussing me. I said that Kermit the Frog would be ashamed of him if he could see him now. And believe it or not the kid shut up and began to tear up. Note, that kid will never be Front Row material, no guts. The place responded and this show became a nut house. That afternoon, an independent Television station wanted to do interviews with the name hardcore sheet writers. Meltzer, Keller, Bowdren and Mitchell got airtime. I got the boot.

I was not worthy of airtime even though I was told to be there. Maybe that set the tone for the independent show later. No, that's not true, we always acted that way.

There was this small time manager there with the catchy name Mister Fritzie. During his match he sawed his head off for our enjoyment. This guy bled buckets and after his match I saw the surreal image of Mister Fritzie with his head wrapped up in gauze and blood standing next to Dave Meltzer trying to get a big break. I pointed this out to Bruce and we agreed it was a strange life Meltzer led. Every nut in the world saddled up to Meltz when all he wanted was to be left alone and watch the show.

God, that was really weird. I will never forget that image.

Then the fun began.

This one crazy woman really got upset with us taking over the show. I can assume this was her home court and she was a face fan. That night the shuffleboard arena was my court not hers. She got so pissed off she started screaming her head off at us. Then she stomped back to her Front Row seat and sat down in a huff. When she sat down her metal seat exploded to the ground! Man, she really got the treatment then. I think she got up and left the show.

There was a match with Bob Cook versus Mister Tits, that's what Bruce called Lou Perez; Bruce being a self-proclaimed expert on wrestling. And the guy didn't like that one bit, Mister T lost it and started to go after Bruce. Usually I would step in and protect the weak but hell it was Bruce, he deserved the beating. I mean, just because this wrestler has big tits due to steroid use is nothing to get riled up over. Think about it, if you get on the juice you should expect a nice rack. Be proud young man! Be proud!

Kill him Mister Tits! No sweat off my back.

Bob Cook came to the rescue and kicked T in the head from the ring. And the wrestling suddenly spilled back into the ring.

You know, I used to like Bob Cook.

This show was an odd collection of has-beens and never-wills. They had a Battle Royal and this freaky six hundred pound guy won. I think his name was Man Mountain Brody. And we all knew the reason this guy won was because if he fell out of the ring he would have died. After the match this huge chick wrestler name Pink Cadillac entered the ring and challenged Mountain. She said—and I quote—"My clit is bigger than your balls!" I hope the children in attendance will be forever wondering just what that means.

Thank God that Florida is not "the show me state."

Oh! And Buddy Landell didn't show for the main event. Landell had a nickname, No Show Budrow, now you know why. Another wonderful day of culture in Florida .

The next morning WCW had the class of having an autograph session for the fans. The best part was Boris Malenko showed up and we all had the chance to talk to him for a while.

Malenko was one of my favorite stars of Florida Championship Wrestling. And he was very nice and patient with all of us. A little later we got the chance to talk with Lance Russell and Gordon Solie. That was another real special moment. Hudson, Prazak and I grabbed up a chance to talk with Bob Roop for about an hour. Roop was a tremendous wrestler all through the seventies and he was really honest and funny with his memories of Florida . What a super time we all had.

That night was the Flair versus Fujinami card and I was not disappointed. The guys from Florida got us Front Row seats right behind the announcing team of Tony Shavanto and Dusty Rhodes. TV viewers at home turned in to the Pay Per View and there was Greensboro's finest with a sign reading, "Front Row on Tour!" It must be fate right?

We had a ball at that show giving Dusty shit all night. For me that was the American dream, the freedom of lighting up Rhodes for three hours.

The show had the amazing site of the first appearance of Jim Herd's latest creation, Oz.

This was a total bomb right out of the gate. As soon as Kevin Nash took off his rubber mask some kid near me said, "Aaaaahh, that is not OZ! That is that stupid Master Blaster!"

From the mouth of babes comes the truth.

That crap was really funny. Think about it. A company worth about a billon dollars came up with this shit and thought that we would buy it. Well, a ten year old wouldn't believe it, that's for sure.

We also got to see a great match with Luger and Sting versus the Steiner Brothers. Those guys did a super job of using each other's finishing moves on the other. It was a hard-hitting match, the best on the card.

Then came the main event with Flair versus Fujinami. It was a great match too. Both guys worked their tails off. There was one bad moment when they both went for the double bridge move and missed it badly. I think that was the first time Flair had ever shown his age by missing a move. It was a super weekend of graps and I wish you all could have been there.

At the airport getting ready to go back home we ran into the Sting family. Sting had warmed to the Front Row over the years and he had his wife, family and infant son was with him. He waved us over and we talked about the show. He was a nice guy even if I always thought of him as Stink.

As we boarded the plane, Sting stopped me. He was sitting in first class and wanted to know what I thought of Flair's match. I said it was really super. He told me Flair was really worried about it, he didn't think it was as good as it should have been. This demonstrated just how much Sting cared about the business. He really wanted to know what I thought of Flair's match, not his. It was also fun giving him hell as he walked his crying son up and down the isle trying to get the kid to sleep.

Look at daddy Sting! Aaaahhh! Isn't he cute!

Man, that was a hell of a trip.

On Tour: The Meadowlands

The inside scoop was that Flair was going to win the World Title back from Sting at the New Jersey Meadowland show. Perfect timing for me, I was already going to be in New York for the mammoth Comic Book Convention in Manhattan .

In times like these I knew there was a rasslin' God looking out for me. The Comic Book show was really super but I had to figure out a way to get to the New Jersey for a match without taking a cab. That's serious cash my friends, taking a cab that distance. I rode the hotel shuttle for ten bucks to the airport. I knew the Airport Hilton would be close so off I went. As we drove into New Jersey it started to sleet and snow. I freaked out. But this was for a Flair title change so I sucked it up.

Arriving at the airport the damn place was a inundated due to the weather, people were crawling the walls trying to get out of town. At this point it was impossible to get a cab to the hotel. There was a line fifty people deep waiting for a ride out of this hellhole. So I started looking around and I spotted the Hilton lights outside.

Man, I can walk that distance easily so like a dumb ass I took off through the snow and sleet towards the hotel. This would be a cool move in North Carolina but in the frozen north things are not as close as they seem. I am walking for about a mile when I realize that this is really stupid. It was not the distance but the eight-lane highway I had to cross in this shitty weather. I still get cold writing about this. I finally hit the hotel parking lot and sloshed my way into the hotel lobby. I am covered in snow when I get in and who is standing there laughing at me but Sting. Sting takes one look and waves me to the front of the hotel check in line. He is laughing his ass off and says, "Hey, did you walk all the way from Greensboro ?"

It felt like it, trust me.

Sting wanted to know why I was here and I was not going to tell him I knew the finish and he was going to do the job and drop the title. I just said, "Aaahh, I am a big fan!"

Man, is that a lame lie or what?

I don't think he bought it but I didn't want to jerk the guy around. Looking back I should have said, "Hey dude, I came all the way from Greensboro to see you do the job. I mean you ain't drawing and you ain't making any cash for the company so I came to see the Nature Boy rule!"

But, I didn't do that for some reason.

After along wait, and I do mean long, Bruce, Wade Keller and K.C. showed up so I could throw my stuff into the hotel room. We got to meet a lot of wrestlers on that trip. Luger was excited that we were there, he introduced us to the Stieners and Tom Zenk. Why do I always have to meet Tom Zenk anyway? Why can't some one introduce me to Terry Funk or Buzz Sawyer? It is always Tom fuckin' Zenk.

Lots of hardcore fans showed up for this event at the Meadowlands. Meltzer called a limo service, this was such a good idea that Mike Gunner did the same thing. There were at least ten guys going so when the two limos showed up, we all piled in the first one and took off.

The second limo driver didn't know what to think.

"Hey man, I think Tom Zenk needed a ride."

If ever anyone asks what the worst pain in the world is I usually answer kidney surgery. The second worse is riding to the Meadowlands with Mark Madden sitting on you. Madden is a really nice guy but the guy is a load. Trust me, I know.

Well, as we made our way to the show we all noticed that a lot of people were wrecking their cars on the highway. The weather was brutal. In an instant, right in front of the limo, a Volkswagen was doing an eight sixty. Meltzer said that if there was a wreck and everyone got killed that there would be no more newsletters left in the world.

A sobering thought. "Slow down Ace! Slow down!"

I doubt with all the traction we had with Madden, Gunner, and Jimmy Suzuki in the car that we had anything to worry about.

The weather really did a number on attendance, as a result the show was only a third full. For the first time Meltzer got us all comp tickets. Well, it was the first freebees I ever got for a show. And what great seats, second row right behind Beth Flair! She was very cool and actually thanked us for being there. I felt sorry for her because she was sitting next to those strange Red Beret security people from New York. We all knew those people were nuts but, then again, look at the example I was setting.

There was a mixed match with Lex Luger teaming with Lawrence Taylor in a football match. This was right during the NFL playoffs and the Giants were on their run to the Super bowl. Very strange that the New York Giants would allow something like this to happen but I doubt they even knew it .

Then came the Flair versus Sting match and sadly Sting mailed it in and did nothing for the match. Even the immortal Ric Flair couldn't save that one, a real stink bomb. I was very disappointed in Sting for not respecting the title or Flair, I will never understand that.

On television when they showed the title change you could see all of us sitting there. I could imagine the people wondering what the Front Row was doing in New Jersey?

The newsletter elite went backstage to talk with the stars. but I was told I could not go back. That was fine with me but I was getting tied of being treated so rudely by people that should know better. So I went out in the goddamn cold and flagged down the limo. Believe it or not the limo driver did come back and was circling the arena. I told the driver to wait, that the guys would be out soon. It was a long soon. I bet I was out there for at least an hour driving around the building. Just as the limo driver had me convinced that the other guys had gotten a ride with someone else, I spotted Wade and Bruce hiking through the foot of snow trying to find us. All the guys then piled in and once again, I got the Madden Crunch. Now I know why I don't have any children.

It was difficult trying to get out of there but we then went to Lawrence Taylor's bar to hang out. That wasn't a whole lot of fun either because they were not serving food and the wrestlers were in the upstairs VIP room so it was a pain getting a chance to talk to them.

New Jersey is no paradise to me.

Clearing the Air

I will protect no one in this column, excuse me as I unzip my head and let all this spill out on you.

One of the funniest things I ever saw was back in the old Mid-Atlantic Days when this redneck was sitting with his family of six kids and he was furious at Paul Jones for cheating at ringside. This guy was so hot he stood up and confronted Jones with his fists. Paul Jones stepped back made a hand signal and two cops ran to ringside to pick this guy up and carry him out of the building with his legs kicking in protest. All of his children were running after their father yelling, "Daddy! Daddy! We want to watch the show! Daddy, we want to stay and watch the show!"

The best use of a sign that I lettered written by someone other than me goes to Richard Skinner. Sid Vicious was walking out to ringside and turned to yell at some fans when Skinner held up a poster right in his face that read, "I HATE YOU!"

Sid was totally speechless but the sign spoke for everyone in attendance.

There was this one person who we called the Ring Master because he wore this large ring and nervously would spin it on his finger whenever he talked to you. One night as the show was ending, Mark Way and I were leaving ringside and spotted under the hanging walkway the Ring Master with a tourniquet around his arm shooting up heroin. He seemed very proud of himself.

To the right of the ringside end zone sat a bunch of Front Row wannabees., Bobby R. Yates, Todd, Chuck and Mr. Smiley, and some others, I can't remember their code names. These guys would make the worst signs in the history of wrestling and think that they were really funny. One night they made a sign that said, "Dutch Mantel looks like Cousin It of the Addams Family!"

Not only was it not funny it looked like it was lettered by a five year old. The letters were less than a half an inch high and could not be read unless you were about two feet away. That night I was prepared and held up a sign that read in huge letters, "THEIR SIGNS SUCK!" With an arrow pointing at them.

I know. I have no shame. You could hear the crowd roll backwards with laughter as everyone began to read my message.

One night we lost our coveted seats and had to sit front row in the end zone. Turns out the wannabees got our seats. And believe this or not they dressed just like the Front Row! They were all dressed in Hawaiian shirts and one of them was wearing a straw hat just like me. They thought they were funny and could fool the wrestlers with this disguise.

One problem. They looked like idiots and everyone knew it. Tony Schiavone walked out, took one look, and shook his head in disbelief. Tony walked down to me and stated, "You know, I have seen a lot of strange things in this business and that is one of the strangest things I have ever seen. What is the problem with those people?" Can you imagine fans dressing up like fans? Well it happened.

These usurpers decided to go with their own name—The Shiites. Well, they almost spelled it right.

On one occasion a big redneck walked up to me on the Front Row and wanted to buy one of my signs so he would look cool. He was very serious about this so I told him I would trade him one for his cowboy boots. He wouldn't go for the trade so I made a counter offer and asked for his silver belt buckle. I wanted to see if this knucklehead would spend the rest of the night holding up a sign with one hand and holding his pants with the other. Still, no deal.

Finally I sold him one for ten bucks. That was the happiest guy I ever saw at the matches.

When we would leave the show usually we would just throw our signs on the coliseum floor. Then we started to notice at the next show other people holding up our old signs. From then on we kept them and trashed them at a later date.

In Raleigh, we started giving Sid shit about standing next to a jobber. Sid thought we meant that he was a jobber. Man, was he hot! Sid, in a textbook Roid Rage, ran over to Obin and KC O'Connor and blew his nose on them. Both their arms looked like a giant prehistoric slug died on them. Now that was really nasty.

I needed a hot dog with Chile and mustard after that one.

One night Super Star Billy Graham was wrestling Wahoo McDaniel and Wahoo hit Graham with a huge glancing chop. Graham decided to spit at that moment. It was a world-class lougee that went straight up into the air! This thing was real heavy and almost broke free from gravity. Suddenly, this wad turned at its peak and surprisingly did not burn up in re-entering. Then in a once in a lifetime shot this hulking thing landed in this old woman's drink that was sitting on the front row! This old lady looked at this thing swirling in her drink distastefully. Carefully, she stuck her hand in the cup, wiped out the snot missile and then took a drink and started yelling at Graham.

Now that is a real wrestling fan.

The WWF decided to go to Greensboro during the early WCW days. That was the first time I ever saw Hulk Hogan in person. That jerk came walking into the arena that hosted matches by Flair, Valentine, Race, and he's wearing a big plastic hat with a fist on top. I guess he was selling a stupid children's hat or he masturbates a lot and is real proud of it. That was when I knew that all the WWF wrestlers were clowns that suck.

Dudes with Shiite Attitudes Respond

Upon reading the latest column by John Hitchcock, I realize that he is the person I always thought he was. Bad.

On July 8, 1990 in Baltimore, MD, the Dudes with Shiite Attitudes were born. With inspiration of Steve Simms and Jeff Mullins, we became THE act of class in Greensboro, NC.

Never wore a Hawaiian flowery shirt, but we did get a few ribs. Like the time I started a chant to the Angel of Death as he fought PN News. I started, "dough baby dough". AoD picked up on it, said it himself and our friends across the way (as we were not sitting in our usual Front Row Section E seats) picked it up.
And let's not forget the time that "Stunning" Steve Austin made his debut with his former stripper wife, Jeanne Clarke. I pulled out a $20 bill and waved it chanting "dance Jeanne dance" to her. She, of course, didn't like it and went to the other side of the ring where she was met by, you guessed it, Section D doing the same.

The word Shiite was spelled that way as I just wanted to not be too closely affiliated with the terrorist sect. So it was intentional. We had great times in Greensboro. Maybe we were funny, maybe we were not. But we did treat people (the fans) like people and not objects for ridicule. As I said, we were THE class act in Greensboro.

- Bobby Yates

I just read this latest article by John Hitchcock and wanted to make a correction.

He mentioned that someone had a sign that said "Dutch Mantell Looks Like Cousin It from the Addam's Family". John's memory must be getting bad because that was not how the sign read. I made the sign & the only thing it said was "Cousin It" in large (not 2 inch tall) black letters as he stated. I admit that I made an error by spelling Itt with only one 't' and John did point this out at the show.

Why John wanted to run our section in the ground and ridicule us is beyond me. We've never tried to imitate or impersonate them and we never dressed in Hawaiian shirts. We always got along great with those guys and there was no reason for him to write what he did.

John has written some really great articles but this one was totally uncalled for whether he was serious or not.

Hitch responds: Well, that did it, no more rasslin' for me, from now on I'm going to watch Women's Figure Skating and watch reruns of 'Highway Patrol' starring Broderick Crawford.

More Clear Air

Everybody's got something to hide except me and one Mulkey. Once again I start out with the immortal words, everything you read here is 100% true even if some people are in denial.

I only missed two shows from late 1985 to 1991 and the reason was I got real sick and was in the hospital with kidney failure. If being on dialysis is not a good enough excuse for you fine folks then I will pray for you later this evening.

This was around August and September of 1986 but I still watched TV and kept up with the action. The gallant Front Row went on without me keeping the wrestling pot hot but I did return. That was a scary time, if anyone got tough I doubt I could have knocked over a feather. (I received a kidney transplant in 1988 and am now fine under proper medication.)

As we all walked into the Coliseum carrying a bunch of posters the fans began to boo me. They gave me the ultimate salute that night and of course I gave them a wave thanking them for their hatred of all that is wrong with the world. Well, what was wrong in their small grappling world. The Front Row couldn't believe it, we were all shocked at the warm out pouring of, well, pure hate.

Now I knew how Bobby Shane felt. I guess if you wear a hat, make a bunch of heel signs, sit on the Front Row and make people angry, then this is what you get.

Another time in Greensboro a face chick wandered into the Front Row. Sitting directly behind me she could not comprehend why we were cheering for the heels. She had a bad blond dye job and was cheering against the Sheepherders. Of course, this opened an excellent opportunity to light her up.

We all loudly cheered on the Sheepherders who, at that time, were not a comedy act. They were the bloody brawlers from Memphis. After the match, the Herders walked up right in front of me and was railing on this loud chick. And I quote, from Butch, "You are a stupid woman! You should be at home, barefoot and pregnant and in the kitchen!" I turned around and said at the exactly same time as Luke, "That's right cousin!"

The Sheepherders looked this chick right in her face and told her, "These are the only good Americans in this whole bloody place!"

Butch put his arm around me and I said, "That's right cousin! She is bloody stupid!" Man, that set her into a lather. The Sheepherders stood back and gave the Front Row a salute. You could see the guys laughing all the way to the back. That chick was never seen again.

There was a match with Doctor Death Steve Williams versus Captain Mike Rotundo during which both guys were locked up in the corner nearest to us. I yelled out very clearly, "Better watch out Dr. Death, Blackjack might introduce you to his good looking daughter!" Cappy Mike started laughing, totally breaking character. He was hopping on one foot with Death holding him and he was yelling at Death, "Cover for me! Cover! Cover for me!" They then fell into the corner laughing insanely. It took a while for Cappy Mike to get a grip on himself and start wrestling. He then gave us that look like, "Man, don't ever do that again." Did I tell you Mike Rotundo was married to Blackjack Mulligan's daughter?

We got Dr. Death too. This was right after the NCAA threw the book at Oklahoma and his old coach Barry Switzer. Dr Death was matched up with Black Bart so we all heckled Williams. When he was being introduced we began to chant, "Nebraska" at him. Dr. Death was running in place saying, "No way!"

We had his attention so we peppered the guy with NCAA investigation lines. Death was hanging in there until somebody yelled, "Did you get credit for mowing Switzer's grass?" Dr. Death totally lost it and began laughing so hard that Black Bart got pissed and threw his ass out of the ring to get him to stop laughing. Death was gone at that point and Bart kept throwing punches and kicks on him to get him to stop laughing. Nothing worked. Bart looked at us and said, "Hey guys! Stop! I am trying to keep my job!" There was Dr. Death on all fours just laughing and there was nothing Black Bart could do to stop him.

Ah, the match really sucked. I gave it four stars.

G.L.O.W in Greensboro

The Gorgeous Ladies Of Wrestling made an appearance at the Greensboro Coliseum and it was a hoot. Except every GLOW wrestler except one was a fake. This was a major disappointment because, well, the girls on the national telecast show were very, very hot young ladies. I have a pulse, right?

For the uninformed, GLOW was like taking a wrestling card and mixing in Hee Haw. The show did have a sense of humor about it in that it didn't take it self to serious. That is why it worked. That and the hotties dressed in sexy wrestling gear. Do any of you remember the old Apter Wrestling magazines with the oddly placed "apartment wrestling" features? That was a S&M flesh fest that kind of was a turn on if you had never seen a Playboy.

The feature would have two young girls wrestle sometimes in their underwear and a photographer would take sexy angled pictures of the struggle. Believe it or not, there was even a referee counting the falls if that ever happen. Aaahh, the fifties fetish fan must had a field day with this stuff. I have to admit I liked it too. But where were the photos and articles about Ernie Ladd versus Rufus R. Jones feud?

Anyway, about 5,000 folks showed up for this "shake down the rubes" of a show. The girls did try to put on a good performance. As I remember they had about four or five bad matches. The thing that drove me crazy was these replacement wrestlers used the names of the girls on TV but nobody bought it. There was a good crowd pop when Colonel Ninotchka came out and you could tell she was not the hot girl from television. Everyone there was very disappointed and felt ripped off.

But one real GLOW girl did show, it was reining champ Mercedes. Now ladies and gentlemen that girl was beautiful. She came out to warm up the crowd about half way thru the show. She smiled and asked everyone to show her your muscles and flexed her bicep. Every kid in the place stood up and flexed for this goddess. Mercedes then turned to my side of the ring and asked to see our muscle. I stood up and said no problem and started to unbutton my pants.
Mercedes half laughed and screamed and turned her back to me from then on.

A little later they had the main event with Mercedes in a tag team match versus who knows and who really cares. They did a spot where one of the girls put a banana split move on Mercedes and she was turned perfectly towards yours truly. You know what? She was not wearing any underwear under her tights and nothing was left to your imagination. Just a note to real wrestling fans, most female wrestlers wear type thick stockings under their trunks. But if the girl is really young and hot, they well; they just wear as little as possible. And if you really think about it, wasn't that what GLOW was selling away?

I have seen Starry Night by Van Gogh and a few Vermeer and Rembrandt paintings but this was a sight worthy of any museum in the world. And about a hundred people took pictures for later proof and enjoyment.

Mercedes left GLOW when it crashed and burned then had a solid wrestling career in the WWE. I loved the production but the wrestling sucked. What the hell is wrong with me?

Ghosts from Wrestling Past

Times were tough for the old WCW in the late-eighties, it seemed that most of the quality wrestlers left or were fired.

It was a real bitch to be a fan and see Greensboro's crowds drop off. I had gone to Baltimore one last time and witnessed first hand the destruction of the great Mid-Atlantic territory. An infamous show where Ric Flair left for the WWF and I watched a stunningly bad championship match with Lex Luger versus Barry Windom. This was a program that is still considered by most fans as the worst ever. There was a lot of fan hatred for a promotion that really didn't give a shit.

Security was attempting to locate and destroy all the negative signs in the crowd. Remember, at the start of a show the announcer would ask everyone to hold up their signs to "See how creative they are." It was a trick to confiscate the signs they didn't like.

I snuck in a poster that said, "WE WANT FLAIR!" and hid it under Big Eddie. It really got the fans going when I stood on my chair and started them chanting for Nature Boy. I know this got over the noise sweetener because a lot of folks said they heard it on the Pay-Per-View.

There were two other memorable moments in this show. First, they had a lumberjack match and walking to ringside was P.N. News wearing a T-shirt and cut-offs. He looked like a wreck and some guy yelled right into his face in a Yankee accent, "NEWS, YOU FAT FUCK!" News just stood there in his flip-flops like the fat fuck he was and I laughed my ass off.

Second, the next morning I witnessed at the bar Dusty Rhodes and David Crockett toasting and celebrating their freedom from Ric Flair. And I can tell you this, David Crockett looked at Dusty like he was his long lost girlfriend with stars in his eyes. Which struck me as very creepy. These two guys were really happy that Flair was gone and it made me sick. This is another reason why I hate Dusty Rhodes and you should too.

At the next Greensboro card I had a brainstorm. The main event was a cage match with five on five. It had sinker written all over it. When all of these grapplers walked toward the ring we put bags on our heads.with the names of all the great talent that were gone from the promotion. Flair, Blanchard,

Arn Anderson, Hawk, Animal, Jim Cornette, Stan Lane, Bobby Eaton, Steamboat, Buzz Sawyer, and a few others I can't remember but you get the drift.

Then I held up a large sign that read, "GHOSTS FROM WRESTLING PAST!" We all were moaning like ghosts haunting the Coliseum. I think I was under the Arn bag. When Kevin Sullivan and Sting came out they totally lost it laughing. Sullivan took a look and screamed laughing, "That's Funny! That's Great!"

Tom Zenk walked over and shook my hand saying, "Come on guys, Get Serious! This is wrestling!" I think that was the most entertaining thing Zenk ever did in his career.

The match was a laugh fest, the wrestlers couldn't keep a straight face the entire time. I wonder what all the Marks thought of this?

Yeah, like who cares?

When Black Bart finished his match, he rolled out of the ring and said directly to us, "Aaaahh, cold beer!" Words the big man really believed in.

What kid wouldn't want to be
Ric Flair on Halloween?

Jerry Allen and the WWF

The WWF had a house show in Winston-Salem one night in 1988 and a few of the Front Row crew decided to check out the competition. Obin, Big Eddie and yours truly jumped into my car and made the thirty-minute trip.

We had gotten lucky with Front Row seats as the place was about two thirds full. The first thing that really stood out was that the ring in the WWF is very small compared to the Mid-Atlantic Wrestling rings. It looked like a playpen instead of a ring and it was about half the distance to the floor. This visual made the wrestlers look a lot larger and taller and I was stunned just how bad the wrestling was in person. Most of these guys did a planned routine that was real bland.

The first match was Outback Jack versus some jobber that I cannot remember. I really try to forget the painful things in my life. This was one that I could not shake. Out House Jack was a big guy from Australia and his music was that crappy song from down under, Tie Me Kangaroo Down Boys!

I decided to light this guy up and really started in on him. Within three minutes Jack blew up bad and after the match he walked over to me to ask, winded, and asked me if it really was that bad?

Yeah, it was.

Then in the middle of the show out walks this job guy named Terry Gibbs. Gibbs was a very valuable hand for the WWF for about ten years. He wore these really cool black leather boots with black knee protectors. I figured this was the "bore the fans before the Hulkster match." This was the "bring the crowd down" match that would grind down the action so the fans could get some pizza or a drink and have a bathroom break.

Why they did this crap was a great mystery to me personally because all the matches so far bored me and couldn't they just bring out Out House Jack again? That would do the trick. Well, out of this mess I decided to give Gibbs some ribbing. I yelled out at him, "Hey, is this the bore the fans before the Hulkster match? What did we do to deserve this? We are already bored with this crap!"

I really hit a nerve with that line because it was the truth and Gibbs was in a mood to play. Terry Gibbs just exploded across the ring and started to scream at me. He wanted me to sign a contract to fight him in the ring. I told him that I wanted to start at the top not the bottom so I couldn't wrestle a jobber like him. That would be a step down in my career goals. After all, he had never won a match on TV so what was in it for me?

Then out to the ring came Gibbs opponent, another loser name Jerry Allen. I had a field day with that! I told Gibbs if he could beat Jerry Allen then he could have a match with me. But I called his opponent, "Jerr-RAY Allll-en!"

This back and forth between Gibbs and myself went on for the whole match. Gibbs attacked Allen and worked him over for about three or four minutes and the whole time he continued to banter with me. He then knocked Allen out of the ring and grabbed a hold of referee Earl Hebner. Gibbs then yelled, "This old man could even kick your ass!"

I went off yelling, "Personally I think Hebner could kick your ass! The guy is great at his job unlike you!"

Suddenly, a bunch of other fans tried to get in on the action and began to heckle Gibbs too. He would have none of it. He looked at this loud mouth with a New Jersey accent and screamed, "I am yelling at this jerk, not you, so sit down asshole"

As this went on, Jerry Allen climbed up on the top rope, was waiting for Gibbs to turn around. I saw what was going to be the big finish and I told Gibbs to turn and face his opponent because he could not face me until he beat Jerr- Ray Alll-en.

Gibbs turned around swearing at me and was hit with the cross body for the pin. The place went nuts cheering, It was a perfect moment and I started counting with Hebner one, two, three right at the defeated Gibbs. Gibbs sold this like he had just lost a championship match, which made it even more hysterical. Then Earl Hebner ran down to me at ringside and held up my hand declaring me the winner! Hebner looked at Gibbs and said, "The Winner! He kicked your ass and I could too!"

That my friends is making something out of nothing. And people say there's no such thing as magic.

There was an intermission and when they came back to start the matches again, Earl Hebner came up to me and said, "Terry said he had a blast and we need to do that again real soon!"

I told Hebner to say to Gibbs that it was a great time and I would be game anytime. Is that cool or what? Gibbs knew I was working him as hard as he was working me.

The main event was Ricky Steamboat vs Randy Savage and it was just like their Wrestlemania Three match. I started in on both of them. I could not understand how these two guys could take a back seat to Hogan. They were ten times the wrestlers of that over-rated jerk but I got no reaction from either of them.

Another night, another adventure, if you ever see Big Eddie or Obin you can ask them about it.

Welcome Home Arn

Word was that Arn Anderson finished out his WWF contract and would be heading back to WCW. This was a part of a WCW screw up when Tully Blanchard didn't sign to return due to a short payment screw job. Arn did sign and was set to return in a TV taping in Greensboro .

At that time WCW began this stupid run, taping all the television shows in Greensboro. It was a blast for a while being on TV all the time but the crowds began to thin out and the Greensboro attendance began to hit the two thousand range. That was really sad to see.

It was just a matter of time before WCW stopped running in my hometown. For years Greensboro was the hot bed of the Mighty Mid-Atlantic and now was dying a painful death right in front of my eyes. It got so bad that some fans began calling me up to see if the Front Row was going to be there and that began to be the determining factor if some fans ever went to the show. Now that is sad.

All was right with the world this night because Arn Anderson was wrestling for his fan base at the Greensboro Coliseum. Everybody was really fired up for the big return, Arn's first opponent was the Great Bob Cook. Bob Cook was the guy who saved Bruce's life down in Florida on the shuffleboard court from the evil Mister Tits.

The TV taping began with a coming next match shot with Arn standing on the ring apron looking around. From behind him you saw a poster that said, "WELCOME HOME ARN!"

The was just a squash match but both guys wrestled a solid set. Cook started by slapping Arn in the face. Arn stopped, looked right at us on the Front Row, then looked at Cook. All hell broke loose as Arn started kicking the shit out of Cook.

Then suddenly Arn says loudly, "I have somebody I want to introduce you to!" Arn threw Cook right on the floor in front of us. He lifted Cook, held him up, and told him to, "Read that sign." He could plainly see the 'Welcome Home Arn' sign, big as life. Then Double A smashed Cook into the barricade right in front of us. The really funny thing was hearing the commentators remarking about what was happening. Jim Ross said something about there being a lot of Horsemen supporters around here. And Gordon Solie then added, "Yeah, right where it says, WELCOME HOME ARN!"

A little later as both wrestlers were back in the ring, Arn made it a point to turn towards us and say, "It's great to be back home!"

Why Me, Lord? The Eric Watts Story

The Greensboro Coliseum's wrestling days were numbered by 1990. I think we got down to a crowd of 1,800 to 2,000 a show and that just wasn't enough. WCW was ready to pull the plug and sadly we all knew it. So the good old Front Row started to have fun stirring up the mix.

Bill Watts was now running the company; he was in a very tough spot because his job was to cut costs and contracts. Watts had a reputation of being a smart booker but asking wrestlers to take less money is not a good job to have. And bringing in his son as a top star wrestler was a really stupid idea. Eric Watts was a tall thin quarterback from Louisville who didn't know how to wrestle but was pushed down everyones' throat like he was the second coming.

He sucked and everbody knew it. How badly? Think Angelo Mossca Jr. bad.

Word got out that Watts was on a big winning streak, he would wrestle and defeat Arn Anderson in Greensboro. This was like Michael Jordan being soundly defeated one on one by Ray Charles. And, for the record, Ray Charles is both blind and dead.

Anyway, that really pissed everybody off and I decided Arn was not going to lose to Eric Watts. There was no way this was going to happen. I made plans to stop this insanity. I went up to a friend of mine named Tarron Coleson who wrestled on the independents and hired him to do a run in during the match. I told him that when Watts was going for his finishing hold the STF, he would then jump into the ring and stop the match. I was willing to pay Coleson two hundred bucks and post his bail if he got thrown in jail.

And he said he would do it. I didn't have two hundred but Coleson didn't know that.

Tarron was a big boy, about six two and about 380 pounds, I figured that he could take the beating he was going to get by diving into the ring that night. But then, if you can't take advantage of your friends, who can you take advantage of?

Word got around that Arn doing the job to Watts was not acceptable and people got to talking. In the Pro Wrestling Torch it was reported that if Arn lost to Watts that there would be a riot. Then we all began to hear reports that Arn Anderson was hurt and would not wrestle in Greensboro that night. That was fine with me but as the matches neared it was on and off again about Arn appearing.

The big night came and out walked Watts to the biggest blasting of all time. He strolled out with David Crockett and four Greensboro policemen ready to rumble. It was a very surreal moment... but then who walks out to face Watts but Stunning Steve Austin!

Yeah, it was that Steve Austin in the curtain jerker no less.

As Austin began his walk to the ring we all chanted, "We Want Arn!" That didn't go over very well with him. Austin was yelling at the Front Row and pushed the steel barricade at us.

Just as quickly we all pushed the barricade right back at him. It was not the smartest thing to do, the cops began to walk towards us and Crockett said, "Go on! I always wanted to throw your ass in jail!" Then, as if by magic, Austin defused the situation by climbing into the ring. The match was on and poor Austin did not look happy having to lose to this over-rated punching bag Eric Watts.

This match went about ten minutes when, near the end, Austin was trapped in the STF finisher and made the ropes. Watts put the hold on again and believe it or not the time expired and the match was a draw. As Austin left the ring, we all began to chant, "Austin Rules!" Steve looked over at us and smiled a huge sigh of relief. Austin gained everyone's respect that night and Watts looked like a real chump standing there in the ring dumbfounded without his hand raised.

We found out later that Steve Austin got into big trouble for not doing the job to Eric Watts. Bill Watts called him into his office in Atlanta and asked why. Austin told him that he couldn't lay down for his untalented son in front of such knowledgeable fans. That would make him look stupid.

You know the truth hurts.

We were not rid of Eric Watts that easily, he returned a few more times to punish us with his idiotic push. One night I made a sign on typewriter paper that said, "Eric the Weenie" on one side and a hot dog on the other.

I took this ugly thing down to Kinko's and printed up about three hundred of them. When I got to the Coliseum, I started giving them out to everyone. A couple of young kids asked me why I was doing this to Watts, I looked them right in the face and said, "Didn't you hear? Eric Watts turned on Sting and beat his ass in Raleigh!"

That was a lie but it worked! Those kids took a handful and gave them out to everybody. When Watts came out that night, he got the Weenie chant from all two thousand fans in attendance. And man was that funny!

During his match, Watts was being hammered by all of us on the Front Row. Bruce Mitchell stood up and said, "Hey Watts! Is it true you threw four interceptions in that bowl game?"

At one point Watts was thrown from the ring and was right in front of us. I really thought he was going to start swinging at us by this time. But to his credit he slyly looked right at us both and said, "For your information, that was five interceptions!"

And he winked at us.

So I guess he wasn't all that bad a guy. But he sucked as a wrestler.

On Drug Testing....

The World Famous Squeegee Story

There was story going around about Sid Vicious getting embarrassed in a bar by the WCW wrestlers. As the story goes, Sid was in the bar talking trash, that all the small wrestlers in the company should just retire and make room for the taller, bigger wrestlers.

Using the term wrestling and Sid in the same sentence was a great injustice in my opinion. He was steroid huge but never drew a dime and totally sucked as a performer. That was what he was, a performer not a wrestler.

Anyway, the talk became heated when both Brian Pillman and Mike Graham stood up to Sid. These two were short but had big hearts and had had enough of Sid running them down. Sid began to make excuses in the bar saying that he had an injury to his arm and couldn't fight them. This injury looked to be a band-aid so the guys laughed him out of the place.

Sid did return, walking back into the bar with a squeegee demanding a fight. Both Pillman and Graham tussled over who would get the right to kick Sid's big ass and Sid ran out of the bar.

I heard that story and thought it was worthy of a rib, we'd have some fun with it in Greensboro. The day before the match I made some home-made squeegees out of poster board. They were about a foot long and looked pretty cheap but it was the best I could do with such short notice. (I really did go looking around town for real squeegees but I couldn't find any.) I think there was not enough rain that spring and the squeegee crop was decimated. When the other members of the Front Row saw these things they said it was the stupidest idea I ever had and that it was a total waste of time. But I took them with me anyway.

As the card started the opening match had Mike Graham wrestling in it. Graham, the seasoned pro, just blew the whole thing off with no reaction at all.

Then came the tag match with Brian Pillman; the fun began as Pillman was walking to the ring and K.C. O'Connor yelled out, "Hey Pillman!

What would you do if Sid was here right now?"

Pillman looked back and said, "If that big bastard ever shows his face around here, I will kick his big ass!"

During the match, we began to do the tomahawk chop with the squee-gees and began to chant like they do during the Atlanta Braves and Florida State fans do.

Whaaaaaaaaaaaa! Wa! Wa! Wa! Wa!, Wa! Wa!, Wa! Wa! Waaaaaaaaaaaaaaaaa!

Worked like a charm! Most of the fans had no idea what was going on but Pillman really went nuts laughing with us. After his match was over he walked over and asked for a cardboard squeegee to take home. I said no problem and gave him one. Pillman walked around the ring doing the Squeegee chop laughing all the way back to the dressing room.

The night was still young when out walked the world's strongest man, Bill "I can't wrestle a lick" Kazmeyer. This huge muscle bound goon had won the strongest man competition many times and now was going to try to make a few bucks in Pro Wrestling. A few bucks were much more than this slug was worth.

Kazmeyer didn't have a hint how to wrestle a match but WCW thought he would bring over a bunch of crossover fans. Are there fans for pulling a bus or carrying a refrigerator? No, the guy just sucked out loud and everyone noticed.

As soon as he walked into the ring we started giving him shit. Kazmeyer totally lost it and began to curse at us. I asked him if he knew that faces were not suppose to use language like that to the fans? It got worse when he got into the ring to face Lex Luger. Luger was a guy with a million dollar body but I never got the feeling he was ever comfortable being a wrestler. He tried, but he really wasn't that great but he stayed around wrestling for a long time collecting checks. I always liked Luger. At times it is hard to defend that but it is true. Gary Hart was managing Luger.

Well, the match was really slow and really bad. It was funny watching Luger sell all the power moves of Kazmeyer when that was exactly the moves people have been selling for him over the years. Luger would run into Kazmeyer and fall down. Luger would do the test of strength and fall to his knees in pain. And needless to say, selling for somebody is not Lex Luger's strength. The whole match was a mess.

Luger, frustrated, rolled out of the ring and began pacing in front of us. He turned and walked towards me and said, "This match sucks!"

"Yeah, Kazmeyer really stinks," I replied.

No longer in character Lugar said, "This is very embarrassing. I want you to know that on nights like this you will understand why I want to walk away from all this shit!"

I told him, "Hey, we will start cheering and try to make it better."

Luger then says, "Good, do something because this really does suck!"

All during this exchange Gary Hart was horrified but I thought it was real funny.

Lex stepped back into character and started the match again.

It wasn't that long of a match. Luger and Kaz locked up and we all began to chant, "It can only get better! It can only get better!" Lex looked right at me and winked. I knew that meant he was going for the finish. Sure enough Lex trips Kazmeyer and covers him with his feet on the ropes for the three count.

The Front Row exploded with cheers as Luger and Gary Hart walked away. Luger waved and laughed with us. Gary Hart looked like he bit into a hard frozen turd.

Then came the main event.

Cactus Jack versus Sting in a steel cage. Cactus walked out to the ring carrying a white towel and was really working the Front Row. I made a huge Cactus Jack Fan Club Banner and Cactus really loved it. Calmly, Cactus put the towel in his corner and then did his Bang! Bang! Routine and then caught his own spit out of the air.

The guy is all class. Kinda hard to believe he's a New York Times best-selling author but he is.

Sting walks out laughing and Cactus attacked him at ringside. Man, we all went nuts as those two guys started raising hell right in front of us. They fought all over the ringside table and then carried it over into the ring. Both guys were taking huge bumps that night and we all cheered like crazy.

Suddenly, Sting ran to the other side of the ring and began to climb out of the cage. Cactus Jack ran after him and knocked him off the top rope and he crotched himself. Sting sold this nut shot like he got hit with an anvil while Cactus Jack calmly walked over to his corner.

Cactus smiled at the Front Row as he bent over to pick up his towel.

With a quick jerk, Cactus exposed that under the towel was a real wooden squeegee! We all began to scramble for our cardboard Squeegees and began the Squeegee chop! Cactus turned to us and proudly displayed the Squeegee and then began stalking Sting with it.

When Sting turned and saw the dreaded Squeegee he sold it like a shotgun, racing across the ring towards us in fear. It was priceless. Sting was begging on his hands and knees.

Cactus looked at us as we excitedly encouraged him to clobber Sting with the squeegee! Cactus held the squeegee aloft and smacked Sting over the head with it. Sting sold this like he was jumping on a trampoline, once again trying to climb out of the cage to escape the dreaded squeegee.

Cactus beat Sting into the corner and with one arching swing missed Sting, dropping the brutal weapon of destruction. Sting took possession of it and crushed the frightened Cactus Jack, getting the pin.

After the match, Sting laughed as he left the ring. Cactus broke the squeegee and threw it to us as a souvenir. Big Bud Grondy to this day displays his part of the squeegee on his mantelpiece.

Some jerk grabbed the other piece and took off with this small piece of wrestling history.

And in a sad way, it was history. That was the last regular night of wrestling in the Greensboro Coliseum, a history stretching back to the early nineteen sixties.

This is really the classic Front Row story but it has a strange twist of fate. This night could have been one of the reasons that a year later, Arn Anderson and Sid Vicious got in a brutal fight and nearly killed themselves in England. You know that everyone in the back room joked about this night and made sport of Sid at every turn.

It does make you wonder.

Our last night in Greensboro.

ArenaReport

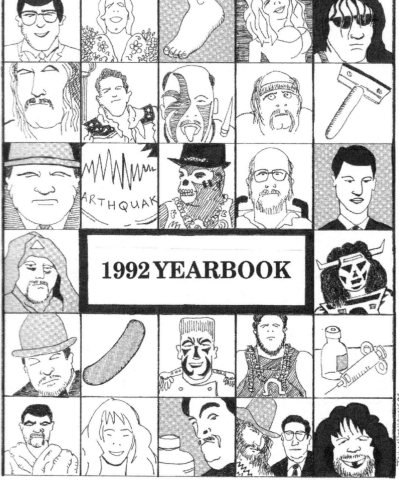

1992 YEARBOOK

Jim Cornette, Ric Flair, Pat Patterson, Lady Blossom, Bret Hart, Jake Roberts, Nature Boy, Buddy Rogers, Hawk, Hogan, Squeegee, Bill Watts, Earthquake, Papa Shongo, Ron Wright, Vince McMahon, Kevin Sullivan, Justin Liger, Mister Fugi, Eric Watts, Sting, Haystacks Calhoon, Juice, Rick Rude, Missy Hyatt, Paul Bearer, Dutch Mantell and Bob Caudle, Cactus Jack Foley.

Stuff Worth Remembering: The New Breed

There are a lot of things that happened in Greensboro that I really should mention. One tag team that stood apart was The New Breed, consisting of two excellent wrestlers, Sean Royal and Chris Champion.

The fact that they were together only a very short period, maybe one year or so, still stings but they made quite an impression. Both guys could wrestle and both held their own in an interview. Why these guys never got a major push still shocks me, they could have replaced the Rock and Roll Express as the hottest face tag in the country.

I don't know if you even remember them but they were very young and athletic in late eighties WCW. They wore these really cool colorful tights and came into the ring to the Beastie Boys song, "You have the right, to fight, to party!" For that time a very hip, current tune and it brought in a younger crowd that WCW had been lacking.

They were never given a chance to catch on. Their first big feud was against the Rock and Roll Express which made sense, booking wise. The old vs the new—these matches were first class and should have been the feud that pushed them up the ladder. But it didn't.

I was sitting Front Row in Greensboro and all the guys loved the New Breed's look and interview skills. We all were wearing Hawaiian shirts and stood and sang the Beastie Boy entrance music. The crowd cheered for the Rock and Roll Express but The Breed really stole the show. And they did it with one move. One move that was one of the ballsiest things I had ever seen.

Chris Champion was beating on Ricky Morton before tossing him to the floor. Pounding on Morton Champion draped him over the barricade railing then ran back into the ring and climbed to the top rope.

It was then that I noticed that the ring had been set up off center with about twenty feet of room to the right side. Champion stood on the top rope ring pole and turned and led us in a chant of, "We Have The Right To Party!"
Champion put one foot on the top rope and one foot on the ring pole and leaped all that distance hitting Morton in the back. Morton sold this move

by flipping into the crowd.

Chris Champion landed on his knees. Let me repeat that. He landed on his knees! Champion and Royal both ran over to where we were sitting and led us in more cheers.

That move still gives me chills whenever I think about it. I still do not know how he did it without getting badly hurt. Champion was wearing kneepads but he landed on solid concrete with no give at all.

To this day I miss those two guys and I wish they had more of a chance to tear more houses down. I remember them having a short run with the Road Warriors and I am sure that with their ability at taking huge bumps, those matches must have been awesome.

Soon after this short feud Chris Champion was in a car wreck where one of his arms was broken. Sean Royal was left on his own as a single but soon left the business. Champion tried to wrestle as a single with the "robot machine" cast but never really got any attention. Champion then went on to other characters but he never really made much of a splash.

In a perfect world we should all be talking about their new DVD collection right now but it was not to be.

The Bloody Independents and Johnny Hunter

As I've stated in the past, I would go to any wrestling card, large or small, and trust me the smaller cards were very strange, very entertaining, and extremely bloody. The violence at these small shows was amazing considering most of the wrestlers got paid very little and had absolutely no chance of making it to the big time. Zero. Zip.

A dream was enough for them.

One day there was this card at Plato's Crash Landing out by the Greensboro airport. Plato's was a country western bar that started to have wrestling nights. The first card was to have the Mighty Igor versus the Man Eating Beast in the main event. Yeah, right, the Man Eating Beast. I hoped he wasn't gay but I had to go. So I got a crew up to see this show of shows and it was a real hoot. Believe it or not, Igor was there in all his glory and the Beast was the independent legend Rick Link doing a strange gimmick with his face painted and on a leash eating raw chicken.

The promoter of this show was the independent legend Johnny Hunter. Hunter was about six feet one and about two hundred and seventy pounds and was built like a beer keg on two pipe cleaners. But he loved wrestling and really did try to bring in the best talent possible for his small audience.

Most of these shows drew about a hundred and twenty people tops. But that didn't stop Hunter from having them even if he lost money doing so. In the seventies Hunter worked as bread man and he sometimes had to pay the wrestlers in day old bread and stale donuts. A lot of very famous people worked these shows. One night, I got to see Austin Idol versus Stan Hansen. This was just after Hansen had left the AWA. I got to talk with Stan and I asked him why he left as champion?

Hansen said, "I couldn't keep my nose far enough from Verne's ass to keep him happy!"

Now that line was worth the seven bucks I paid for front row!

A lot of past and present stars showed up at these shows. Valiant, Morton and Gibson, Bugsy McGraw, Uncle Elmer, and it was a blast.

Johnny Hunter always insisted that he climb into the ring every show and sadly, he really felt that he was letting the fans down if he didn't wrestle.

He was not in very good health and should have never been anywhere near a ring at this late stage of his life. Hunter also ran a small wrestling school and a few people did make it into television. He was most proud of Rick Link and George South who both came through his school and did pretty well.

One other thing about these shows. Every time somebody would blade, hit a major artery and blood would splash all over the place. It was a grizzly atmosphere and not everyone's taste. Of course I loved that stuff but who ever said I had great taste? One night they used a mop to soak up all the blood. It was everywhere.

Another highlight of every Johnny Hunter show was purchasing your ticket from Johnny Hunter. If you had correct change, Johnny would be really relieved. But if you paid with a twenty it would take him fifteen minutes to make change. I am not making this up. The guy really couldn't count very well and wanted to make sure the money was right with both parties every single ticket sold. Johnny had this sweet way off giving back your change and then asking you if it was correct .He would look at you right in the face with those light blue eyes and say, "Is that right?"

Many times I really wanted to fuck with him and bring a fifty but after awhile I told everybody to always bring the correct change. The pressure was getting to Johnny and he had a bad heart so he really needed the fans to help him a little.

At these shows you would see a lot of people who really had no hope of becoming stars. Many of the guys only weighed about 180 pounds and you would look at your friends and shake your head. Of course, I would always hammer them from the front row. That was my job. The main event usually would be scary and bloody. Some fans would not return after witnessing a horrific blade job but I always came back.

One night it was a final bittersweet moment for Johnny Hunter. I think it was in Denton, NC and Johnny had a near sell out crowd. I think there was about 400 plus fans to hit this joint; Johnny never looked happier. He had his biggest turnout ever and stood to make a huge score. Without warning Johnny turned blue then fell out of his chair. He was having a heart attack but everyone in attendance thought he was going to be fine.

This had happened often in the past and, after a few minutes, he would recover.

Not this time.

Johnny never got back up and passed away right on the spot. He was scheduled to have bypass heart surgery later in the week. But he never made it.

His son Tony, who was a referee that night, stayed and continued on the job. There wasn't a dry eye in the house that night.

ME IN 20 YEARS.

A Note from Johnny Hunter's Son

I thought the story on my father was very good. There are just a few things that I would like to add that I know about my father first hand.

As far as him handling the money the way he did, he just wanted to make sure he got it right for himself and the other party. I always remember my father would snap the money when he counted it, to make sure it wasn't stuck together, LOL. But he knew how to count.

As far as him driving a bread truck, it never happened. He did work part time for Krispy Kreme, I even have a wall mounted certificate from the President of Krispy Kreme. A funny story about my father and Brute Bernard; Brute always wanted the creme filled ones, just ask George South, it was really funny.

As far as my father getting in the ring and wrestling; he loved it. I do know that for probably a year before he passed away, he shouldn't have been in the ring. I remember him taking nitro-glycerin pills in the ring. He just loved it so much.

My father always told me, "Tony, if I ever pass away on a wrestling event and it's my show, I want you to run it just like I would have." He would say this when we were putting up rings or postering the towns, etc. He told me this hundreds of times. And on the night of Feb 4th of 1989, it happened. He wouldn't have wanted it any other way. To this day I'm proud of myself for doing what my father asked me to do. His word was his bond.

- Tony Hunter, September 16, 2004

The Bloody Independents,
Diamond Dan and Hoss

I can't tell the whole story of the wonderful world of North Carolina Independent Wrestling with out a mention of Diamond Dan Grondy and Mike Kidd who will be forever known as Hoss from this moment on. Johnny Hunter trained these guys and I in a strange way went along for the ride.

I have been a friend with Dan for many years. He was a part of the early Front Row and is mentioned in the Devil's Triangle story. Hoss is Dan's training partner, which is how I met him.

These two guys are well over six three and 255 pounds. I think that when Johnny Hunter saw them he lost his mind with the possibilities of training these two.

Their first match we all turned out in force to cheer them. Dan was in a two out of three falls tag match. And I think Hoss was on that card too in a singles match. We went crazy cheering for Dan and as he walked to the ring, he picked up the house microphone and started to talk.

This was an historical moment for me because the one thing I knew Dan could do was talk trash with the best of them. His promo was short and very funny. I think. The reason I am not so sure is that the house mic was a screeching, popping mess and you couldn't make out a single word Dan said. (I think all independent microphones suck like that because I never heard a clear one in my life.)

There must be a company somewhere that sells these crappy systems on the cheap to every wrestling group in the Carolinas. It turned out to be historical because it was the last time Johnny Hunter ever let Dan near a live microphone. And trust me, it was a huge mistake because that was really one of his strengths as a performer.

The guy could talk but he never got a chance to explore that talent until he went to Virginia. But that is another story. Dan won his first match winning the last fall. It was a blast and it was the first time I ever really knew a guy who was a wrestler.

Soon after that Dan became the feared Russian Assassin and then he never talked again for Hunter. Hoss wrestled as The Blue Cyclone and he was a natural right from the start. The one thing about Hoss was he had the largest hands I have ever seen.

And he made good use out of them by chopping the shit out of other wrestlers. One night against the Dreaded Bingham Brothers, Hoss chopped one of them and knocked the air right out of the guy. He had to toss the heaving Bingham to the other corner so he could tag but truthfully the other Bingham didn't want to wrestle Hoss so he kind of begged him to tag Dan so he wouldn't die like his brother.

After the match I took a gander at the Bingham Brother's chest and it had this huge red handprint etched on it. That was kind of funny. It was real funny to me, not funny to the Bingham Brothers.

I think I must also add that both The Dreaded Bingham Brothers weighed about one hundred and fifty pounds each. Matter of fact, Hoss performed the very first North American Lucha Libre move at Plato's Crash Landing with a Bingham Brother.

There was a Battle Royal one night and with one hip toss, Hoss threw a Bingham ring over the top rope to the floor. It wasn't planned that way but what a brilliant way to introduce this form of wrestling on the fans in attendance.

Both Dan and Hoss taught me more about wrestling than anybody. In a match, Dan or Hoss would juice and later they would walk out of the dressing room with a small mark on their forehead that looked like a rose bush scratched them! I picked up so much valuable information by just asking and watching. And both guys were always very cool and honest with me.

I owe them both a lot.

The Sting Fan Club

Lets face the facts. Things were getting really, really slow with WCW in the early-nineties. They were now starting to wrestle in Winston Salem, in the annex building. That place only held about two thousand and there were a lot of empty seats, if you get my drift. Leaving Greensboro was a good money saving move but this venue was hell for wrestlers and the fans. Well, not all the fans. I began to warm to this sinkhole. With my loud mouth and the Front Row raising hell, we made the best of it.

But a strange thing happened. We began to like Sting. I know, I know, that is totally against the grain for the Front Row but the guy earned our respect. After his feud with Big Van Vader and the ass kicking he took while losing the title... you had to give the guy a little credit. Was Sting the greatest wrestler of all time? No. But he did try when many just mailed it in night after night.

After the Night of the Squeegee, we decided to mess with Stink, err, Sting and make a positive sign for him.

It was simple," Sting Fan Club!" When he saw it he totally lost it laughing. That's when I flipped it over and it said, "Really." It messed with him more than anything we could have done.

This became a ritual and it always got over with Sting. Stupid signs for Sting were a constant and he would always pop big for them all. One was, "Nice Hair!" for his new dye job.

Mark Way thought up the best sign. Mark was my roommate and kind of liked wrestling. He would never admit it publicly but he did watch every once and a while

We made the Sting Fan Club sign and he was going to wrestle Paul "Mister Wonderful" Orndorff that night. Orndorff had wrestled in that historic feud with Hulk Hogan and had suffered nerve damage to his left arm. This feud was one of the largest moneymakers of all time so he could not take time off to heal so one arm was noticeably smaller than the other.

Well, out comes Sting and I hold up his sign. He started laughing and asked me to turn the sign around. On the flip side I lettered, "GO FOR

THE LITTLE ARM!" Sting was laughing uncontrollably and so I held up the sign for Orndorff who smirked when he read the Sting Fan Club sign.

Then I flipped it.

Believe it or not he broke up too, turned around and walked away. Sting gave me that look like, "You really did it this time." But that was to be expected, right?

Sting looked at Orndorff and said, "They did that, I had nothing to do with it." You had to hand it to Sting, he was a lot smarter than he looked. Orndorff could have killed him if he wanted.

Terry Funk and Signs

As I stated before, Terry Funk is the only wrestler that can be mentioned in the same sentence as Ric Flair. Both men have absolutely nothing in common other than their love and dedication to Professional Wrestling.

Well, it was that time again to get to the Greensboro Coliseum and watch wrestling up close from the front row. We were all in for a treat that night. The main event was Ric Flair versus Terry Funk and that my friends is as close to heaven as a wrestling fan could get.

Then came the question that pops up at every show. How do I get some attention and stir up the crowd. Trust me, with these two guys they needed no help. It was going to be a real classic because both men never, and I mean never, mailed one in. Every match these guys ever had was performed with pride in their art and ability. But, to have a small moment in this match with two of my all time favorite wrestlers, I had to be smart and simple. Then it became crystal clear what to do and what sign to make.

Terry Funk walked to the ring with his then manager, Gary Hart. Why did Funk have a manager? Don't ask me. Terry Funk is one of the greatest interviews I ever heard but old Gary was there anyway. The Front Row was always the first row on a wrestlers right and Funk turned and looked right out at us. I was standing with one sign. The sign was simple and to the point.

It said in big black letters, FUNK IS A PUNK!

Yes, I was taking my life into my hands but I figured on a perfect spot for it. When Funk saw the sign he started walking right towards me and looked directly into my eyes saying, "Funk is a Punk? Funk is a Punk? What the hell is that all about?"

I held the sign arms length towards him and I told him, "Tear up my sign."

Funk, getting closer all the time, said, "What?!?" And I told him quietly, "Tear up my sign, that is what it's there for. Tear it up and it will get you some quick heat. Tear it up."

Funk said," OK, if that is what you want." He took a few steps towards me and with his double cross ranch branding iron destroyed my sign.

I exploded, yelling about how that was my property and he had no right to destroy it. Matter of fact, the whole Front Row was screaming at Terry Funk for ripping up one of our posters. Funk kept walking like a chicken turning his head and barking at all of us.

The crowd reaction was huge! Nobody ever tore up one of our signs before and the crowd went nuts screaming at Terry Funk. Ric Flair saw all this and went to the attack and chopped the shit out of Funk right in front of all of us!

It was incredible how hard they hit each other and we all loved every moment of it. It was wrestling heaven folks.

The match was a four to five star classic. How could it not be? We're talking Flair vs Terry Funk.

The Bloody Independents, Rick Link

I would guess that at ninety percent of the independent shows I attended there was one constant. And that was the disturbing violence of a wrestler named Rick Link.

In every show Link would walk out to the ring and an ass kicking would commence immediately, like clockwork. And it was both his blood and his opponent's splashing out over the ring every show.

Link is about six one and about four hundred pounds and his weight is half above his belt and half under. With his head shaved and hands taped he was one scary looking guy.

The interesting thing about Link, his matches usually lasted about five minutes because of his weight but those minutes would always be riveting. Show after show, night after night, I would look forward to his match because you never knew what would happen.

I know you think I am the world's biggest mark for saying all this but it was the truth. Rick Link was and is a violent guy that often took his problems to the ring and settled them.

These matches were really not shoots because the other wrestlers never seem to fight back. It was just Link making a point that he was the ruler of the back room. Hell, he helped Johnny Hunter train most of the guys he wrestled but he would always lay down a stiff match.

One night in Salisbury, NC at a place we named the Real Cow Palace because it was a stockyard tin building with hay on the floor and cow shit on the metal fence that surrounded the ring, Link wrestled a guy named the Head Hunter.

This Head Hunter was a jacked up body builder, real green. He had a manager and did a little dance for his entrance. Link wrestled this guy very cleanly, up until the finish. Link knocked the guy down then jumped on his back. This took everyone by surprise, nobody saw it coming.

Then Link jumped on the Head Hunter's leg brutally dislocating it. It was one of the most gruesome things I have ever witnesses in 35 years of watching wrestling. They had to bring in an ambulance and take the poor guy to the hospital.

A powerful message was sent that night that Rick Link was the bull of the woods in this little promotion and everybody would have to show proper respect. That was why this was so strange. Everybody always gave Link respect because he trained most of them.

About two weeks later the Head Hunter wrestled Link again, this time Link *broke* the guy's leg. I still don't know what set Link off but I never saw that Head Hunter person again.

One night in Greensboro, Link was going to be in a battle royal. My friend Diamond Dan Grondy, who was wrestling on the card that night, told me to watch Link and Robbie Allman.

Allman had just been on TBS television jobbing and was bragging about it to the guys in the back room. Link was going to kick his ass for talking too much. And he did. Allman entered the ring, the bell rang, and he was in trouble very quickly.

Link grabbed him, hit him in the back so hard Allman doubled over before Link kicked him right in the face with his steel-toed boots splattering Allman's nose all over the ring.

His face was a mess, for the rest of his life he would remember Rick Link every time he looked in a mirror. And then I had to look in the mirror—I was paying money to watch this carnage every month.

Why did Link do this every time he went into the ring? This mean streak that made him hurt so many people? I suspect that he was taught to stand up for himself in the wrestling ring the hard way. Someone must have hurt him very badly when he was a green and starting out.

That may have sent a message that he had to gain the respect of his peers by being ruthless. And it was drilled into Link that you had to always protect the Business at all costs.

Protecting the Business is not something that the old timers took lightly. In this day and age it does seem so stupid to me personally. Because what did the Business ever do for them?

Bad back, shot knees, no future job skills after wrestling, all these things you protect? A lot of wrestlers will tell you that being in front of a crowd being booed or cheered is a type of drug. I understand that completely but chasing the dream has a high price in the small market-wrestling world. I have not seen Rick Link in years but I hope he is at peace with himself.

The Bingham Brothers Return!
(I know you don't know who these guys are)

I got a call from Diamond Dan that he was wrestling Hoss in King, North Carolina and wanted his brother Bud and I to videotape it for him. So asked the obvious question, where the hell is King? He wasn't exactly sure but Bud and I followed him anyway. The independent show was going to be in a seriously redneck bar. Think wrestling ring in Jess Helms asshole and you get the idea.

On the wall was the stuffed longhorn head, right next to it was a dirty bar with about fifty people there to watch wrestling. It turned out that the Bingham Brothers were the promoters of this show and forty-eight of the people there were related to them. We set up the camera on a tripod and were ready for action.

There was plenty of that—and not what we had bargained for. There was a tag match with the Brothers Bingham verse the hated Rose Brothers. The Rose Brothers had been wrestling around these parts for many years and I think they did wrestle in the old IWA for a while.

Needless to say, these guys were really tough and knew what they were doing. Well, scratch that 'knew what they were doing' part. The crowd was very scary because these folks thought wrestling was a real life and death struggle, a crowd made up of uncles, aunts, cousins and second cousins of the Bingham's. They cheered like crazy the whole match. Little did they know what they were in for.

The Bingham's decided that they were going to juice for the first time in front of the home folks but they made one big error. They were scared to cut themselves so they handed the blade to the Rose Brothers to do it for them. Not a great idea.

The match spilled out on the ring floor and one of the Rose Brothers reached down and ham hocked this guy's forehead wide open. The Bingham popped his head right up and the blood shot out everywhere.

I found out later, that when you juice you should keep your head down for awhile to get your bearings and popping up is the wrong thing to do. Man, was it the wrong thing to do!

This guy must have taken fifty aspirin to thin out his blood because he splashed all over the place. Then Bingham passed out on the floor. The other two in the ring went for the quick three count. The match may have been over but the real show was now starting. Suddenly, the entire Bingham Family hit ringside trying to save him, led by the wrestler's mother yelling and crying that her son was dying!

About thirty people hit the ringside yelling and crying, as a group they picked Bingham up over their heads and carried him to the back room for emergency care.

The mother had a towel around his head and blood was smearing all over her and the Bingham brother was like a suffocating carp, flopping around in their arms. After the family members left ringside there was a brief intermission. Man, they needed a break, we all did.

Then this old guy pushed a mop bucket out to mop up all the pieces of Bingham splashed all over the place. There was blood in pools on both sides of the ringside, on the ring apron, all across the ring, even hanging from the ring ropes. And the clean up guy was so bored about the whole thing that it was really bizarre to watch.

Using a towel to get the blood off the ropes the referee at least acted like he cared about what he was doing. Just another day in King, North Carolina for these people.

It still shocks me to this day. Dan and Hoss had a solid match with Dan going over with The Kerry Von Erich/ Ric Flair backslide finish. But I really just remember the Bingham Brothers match. Can you blame me?

And we got it all on videotape.

Heel Time in Thomasville and Burlington

As a group, we couldn't get enough of wrestling. Bruce, Bud, Lisa, Obin, Big Eddie, KC and I went anywhere that was with in an hour and a half drive to see wrestling.

It became our cool thing to do and I bet we all hit every armory and high school gym that had wrestling. And every time we went, we drove the other fans crazy cheering for the heels. These towns were really strange in that these people were ninety percent true believers and we pushed as many buttons we could find.

It was a little dangerous but with that many people in our group, we got away with it. After taking over at the Greensboro Coliseum, these cracker boxes with about one hundred and fifty people didn't have a chance.

We all were loud and obnoxious as any body could be and the wrestlers loved it. The building would be cold during the winter but if we showed up there was heat inside and thee wrestlers played off of us as hard as we cheered against them.

It was a real hoot and after awhile, the other fans broke into two groups. One large group that dreaded seeing us and a small group that wanted to join us.

And if one of these hillbillies tried to sit with us, we would light their ass up as being a turncoat. Man, there were many times that after turning on a young mark I would see the guy leave crying as we hammered the guy .

One night a young guy started cheering with us and I did not like him. So I looked right at him and said he could join our group if he got his teeth fixed. He started crying like a baby.

What a wussy.

Another thing that we all noticed really fast is that every wrestler on the show would have a group of friends' ringside cheering them on.
These people were really easy to spot because once you started giving their boy hell they would pop like nobody's business. This was a lot of fun.
Those guys and gals would get more into yelling at us then cheering for

their buddy.

We got this one chick so hot at us that she went to the back room and demanded that the Lumbee Warrior come out and kick our asses. The Warrior acted all pissed at us but as soon as she turned her back he would laugh with us.

We didn't let anybody join our group but one guy, Chris Cruise. Cruise was the play-by-play announcer for WCW for many years and it turned out he loved wrestling as much as we did.

Of course, he was handicapped because he grew up in Maine and worshipped the WWF product and was the biggest mark in the civilized world for Bruno Samartino.

At first it was very difficult to like the guy because he constantly raved about Bruno. And week after week he got to call the matches at WCW and he couldn't tell that WCW was vastly superior to that over rated Yankee wrestling.

I mean, can you imagine thinking Bruno was a big deal when you watch Ric Flair week after week? But Cruise soon fit right in and we all had a ball at every show we went to.

Cruise also was one of the most out of touch guys I ever met as far as wrestling went. He always asked Bruce and I what was going on in the wrestling world. The guy worked in the business and didn't have a clue most of the time!

But he had a very wicked sense of humor and fit right in. At another show the main event was Bugsy McGraw versus Jimmy Valiant. Mc Graw is a big pot bellied guy and Valiant is really skinny.

Matter of fact, Valiant looked like a homeless starving bum, nothing like the big time main eventer that was so famous in the Mid Atlantic Territory during the eighties. So as the match started, I stood up and announced to the crowd that this match was going to be fought over cheeseburgers.

I then tossed about four McDonald's Cheeseburgers into the ring .I figured that they would put up a real fight for food. Both wrestlers were pretty shocked but Valiant pushed a few burgers into his corner to eat after the match.

The place went nuts cheering against us but that was to be expected. Some did get a laugh out of the stunt.

After about three months we were getting really good heat around all of us. That would lead to other very strange nights in the future.

Hitting the Ring at Plato's Crash Landing

We assembled another crew to go to Plato's Crash Landing for a wonderful night of wrestling, one of the best nights of wrestling I ever went to. I was running my comic book store and talked to every one I could think of into going to wrestling that Friday night.

My catch line was, "It's the most fun you can have with your pants on!" And about two hundred wrestling folks filed in that night. I knew about sixty people in the crowd, for most of them it was their first card ever .

If it is your first night at wrestling you have to really turn it on and the Front Row was primed to raise the roof. And we did just that. The wrestlers that night were a bunch of locals trying to put on a good show. And they needed a lot of help because most of them never should have been in the ring. Personally. I get really tired seeing a bunch of guys trying to act like wrestlers that weigh about a buck seventy-five. It just doesn't work visually but I will say one thing about this motley crew, they did try. There were three moments that really stood out that night.

First, there was a match with Bam Bam Coleson versus Cowboy Chris Star. Coleson I knew from way back because he use to buy slurpees from me when I worked at Seven Eleven.

And he weighed in at about three hundred and fifty five pounds and that is being very kind.

The Cowboy looked like he spent time starving in India and all his synapses didn't fire if you get my drift. We spent the whole match yelling at Bam Bam to pull up his pants.

Then Bam Bam went for the running shoulder block in the turnbuckle on to Chris Star. Chris was a lot smarter than we all thought because he moved out of the way. Bam Bam went right through the ropes, hit the ringside and fell to the floor with an earth-shaking fall. I think that half the audience felt the room shake with that bump. But it wasn't a bump it was a screw up.

Second, there was this guy wrestling named The Flash. That's all I really remember about the skinny guy but he too messed up big time. During the match, Flash tried to walk the top ropes like the Undertaker.

Only one problem, he wasn't the Undertaker. This guy walked about three steps and lost his balance. He fell forward crotching himself on the top rope. I am sure to this day he has never had any children due to this fall.

He then fell out of the ring and began juicing. Hey dude, losing a nut for my five bucks is really enough thrills for anyone to hope for!

The third big moment was not really planned but it really was something that every one there still talks about. Diamond Dan was wrestling in the main event against some guy who looked like a drunken caveman.

Before the main event, Dan told me he was going to win the match with a Hulk Hogan leg drop and he wanted his brother Bud and I to hit the ring and celebrate his big victory.

That sounded cool to me.

So I told Bud and I told my buddy Doug and I told Vic and Brian and Obin and Big Eddie and KC. Well, I told everybody what the finish was and that they needed to hit the ring at the end of the match. I really didn't think that they would tell their friends this but they did and I think about half the people there were primed for the big run in.

You could tell something was brewing, when Dan came out the whole place went nuts cheering him. And sure enough, a miracle happened and Dan won his match with a Hogan Leg drop!

Just as the referee raised Dan's hand in victory the place went berserk, people began flying into the ring from all sides!

It was really funny to look at the tape and see all these people jumping, siding into the ring, cheering for Dan.

One thing that I didn't count on and that was this was a weak ring and as soon as all these people got in it got very wobbly and I could barely stand. It was like trying to stand on a moving trampoline.

Needless to say, Dan was shocked but took it the right way and I raised his hand in wrestling glory.

Or something like that.

The Southern Comfort Boys

It was time for another trip to Plato's Crash Landing for a night of cheap unpredictable entertainment. The usual crew was with yours truly and about 105 other folks were in attendance.

I really loved these kinds of cards. You never, and I mean never, know what you are going to see. Most likely really crappy attempts at wrestling but it seemed every time I went something strange happened. Needless to stay, if I am writing this for your enjoyment, something did.

There was a tag team that night with the Southern Comfort Boys versus the hated Psycho and Man Mountain. Please allow me to introduce these combatants.

The Southern Comfort Boys were two brothers, red headed and in good athletic shape. That was a rarity at these small independent shows, two guy who looked like they could wrestle.

The Psycho... well, that's not really correct. They misspelled his name on the poster, it read "Physo" so from then on he was the Phizzo. This guy was a short fat guy missing his front teeth that did try as hard as he could to put on a match. That ain't saying much in his case but he was entertaining.

The Man Mountain was a 320 pound fat guy that played an insane hillbilly His head was shaved and he wore bib overall in the ring. Think Sling Blade's Carl played by a really bitter, drunk Orson Wells.

The match began and it was the same old stuff until the Mountain went nuts. The Mountain was on top of one of the Comfort Boys and shockingly he reached into his boot and pulled out a steel fork.

Then he stabbed Comfort in the forehead! I think he got in about three or four brutal headshots before the Comfort Boy bolted out of the ring. This was not something that happened every day, seeing a guy get stabbed with a fork. But I guess you know that.

That poor Comfort Boy was bleeding really badly from this attack and began to walk into the crowd to show his wife or girlfriend the head wounds. It wasn't a very pretty sight, that was going to leave a scar for life.

Comfort Boys one and two left the ring really pissed and shocked. Mountain decided to keep going with the match. The Comfort Boy had his back to the ring when Mountain cleavered the poor guy with a steel chair shot to the back of his head. Comfort was hit so hard he traveled four rows deep into the crowd.

I am pretty sure none of this was part of the match and I began to wonder just what caused all this mess.

Was it a battle for back room power? A fight for the book? Did somebody mess with someone's woman? Was it a tussle to see who was the bull of the woods? No, I think the Mountain merely got caught up in the moment and decided to crush this poor guy. Why he chose a steel fork instead of wrapping up a couple of popsicle sticks remains a mystery.

All of a sudden the American Rocker ran in from the back room, tackled the Mountain and pounded him with a flurry of right hand haymakers. I should mention Rocker had a cast on that right hand!

Mountain was nobody's fool. With Phizzo trailing he ran to the back room for safety. A few minutes later, Rocker and the Southern Comfort Boys were running after them and a huge fight ensued. There was yelling, screaming, lots of punches thrown in the back room that night, most of them real. I looked at Obin and Big Eddie—we had to come back for next show. Of course, we did.

.

The Phone Call

Again, it was time for wrestling at the Greensboro Coliseum; this was about 1990-91 when wrestling was really in the crapper for WCW.

The attendance was around 2500 people in a building that held 23,000 so the place looked like a ghost town. It was pitiful but the show must go on so, knowing this could be a bad show, we naturally went anyway.

We are wrestling fans; the few, the proud, we had to go. It is our life.

Sniff, sniff...

We found out through the grapevine that it was Jim Cornette's birthday, a few of his wrestling buddies were going to finish early and get to Charlotte for the party.

The first match was Bobby Eaton versus Cactus Jack Mick Foley and I cannot think of two better wrestlers in the curtain jerker. Both guys wanted to scoot so we decided that, during their match, we would sing Happy Birthday to Jimmy.

I never said that we could sing very well but it truly was a solid effort. And you could hear us clearly. The thing I remember most about this match is that the Front Row seats were full for about five rows and the rest were totally empty. I guess Bobby and Mick took it as a personal challenge to see just how many empty chairs they could knock down during the match. It was amazing to watch these two guys use each other's bodies as bowling balls, throwing each though twenty or thirty chairs at a time. It was a riot to watch and they seemed to enjoy killing themselves for the sad sparse crowd.

After the show old friend Mike Gunter told me he was going to the after-party. Mike gave me Cornette's home phone number and said I should call and wish him a happy birthday. This was a tough call for me to make because I had never met the guy. I had given him a T-shirt and a Parts Unknown hat once but that ain't like calling a guy up cold!

Well, I finally found the courage to call and believe it or not Cornette was happy to hear from a member of the good old Front Row. So happy that he quickly handed the phone to Cactus Jack. / Mick Foley. I was thrilled to talk to him and he told me a very flattering story about the Greensboro Front Row.

Foley told me when he first went to the Mid-Atlantic Territory he was riding to the shows with Larry Zbyszko and Arn Anderson. All of them were bitching about the sad attendance to the shows. And the crowds were really laid back. Arn looked at both of them and said not to worry because Greensboro was coming up soon and both guys began to laugh.

Mick then asked if the stories were true about how crazy the Greensboro fans were? Larry turned around and said that he had a story. At one show he was wrestling a tag team match with Arn and when he tagged in all the fans began to quietly chant, "Stall, stall, stall," it grew louder and louder. He then began to stall and said those crazy fans popped like crazy cheering him for doing nothing!

I remembered that night—it was funny to watch the ultimate stall master at work. I think Larry could do more with nothing than any man alive. Or was he just lazy?

Then Larry said that Greensboro was Arn's town. Arn, who was driving, smiled and told us he loved Greensboro and those fans with the signs really were a lot of fun. Turns out most of the wrestlers looked forward to Greensboro on these long road trips, they would all wonder just what the signs would say. Mick Foley then told me that no matter how bad things got that we should keep making those signs because all the guys really enjoyed them. Some of the wrestlers began to bet on who would get the best signs. And Arn always won.

So after that call you know why we kept keep making all those signs. That, and it was so much fun being a minor participant in the action.

One More Shoot!

It was a dark rainy night. The clouds clapped with thunder and I knew the devil was alive and well. This night was a night for murder and car crashes. Blood on people's shirts would be the standard this night. I knew this would be a hell of a night of wrestling.

Well, I wish the above were true.

It would make this story seem so much more interesting. But the truth is that it was like any other night on the independent scene. I think this show was in Ramseur North Carolina. I went with a few of the guys to raise hell and enjoy the chaotic world of wrestling.

That night was the same old same old. Then out of the back came the scuttlebutt that during the tag match there was going to be a real shoot. It turned out that the wrestler named Jerry Price had been running his mouth about working the TV tapings and being a big star to the other guys in the back room. A big head is the wrong thing to have in any dressing room. This, and the fact that Price was black, really stirred the anger and jealously. I am not saying that this was totally a race-motivated attack but looking back I think that it did add fuel to the fire.

We were in for a real lesson in brutality.

It was a tag match with Price and some nobody versus the Ring Lords. The Ring Lords were two juiced up youngsters that could become very dangerous if they are angry. And they were cool during the match but when Price tagged in, it got very violent very fast. The larger of the Ring Lords started to pound on Price. It was a very stiff couple of moments and then Price bailed out of the ring to the gym floor. This was a good idea for him to catch his breath and to attempt to clear his head and figure out just what was happening. Sadly, both the Ring Lord followed him. Price shockingly had not figured out that he was in big trouble and tried to continue the match. He then took about six big right hands to the face.

It was on then and Price then got into a boxing stance. An old man on the Front Row yelled out, "Don't box with a black man!"

He didn't need to worry because Price was already pretty messed up at this point. Price took a couple more hard shots and he then bent down and picked up the concrete and metal pole that was holding up the crowd ring ropes. I think he was going to use this as a weapon but for some reason he hesitated and the Ring Lords crushed the poor guy. Price went as quick as possible to the back room to get his wrestling gear and bolted the place. When he walked passed me, his eye was quickly closing, his lip was very swollen and he was bleeding from his mouth and nose.

The match itself was quickly finished with a schoolboy roll up pin.

I don't remember the rest of the show but I think you can understand why.

Smoky Mountain High

It was time to hit the road and check out the small but very cool Smoky Mountain Wrestling group. I called my friend Jim Cornette and he asked that I please make a few signs for Tracy Smothers.

Smothers was being pushed as the top baby face in this group and needed a little help getting over. If a sign or two could help, I was more than willing to do it, after all that night my friend Diamond Dan Grondy was wrestling on the show.

This TV taping was in Lenoir North Carolina at a small rec center, it promised to be a blast. I had quite a crew with me, Obin, Big Eddie, Mike Gunter, Bruce, and Bud Grondy too. Bud could get a little too excited whenever Dan wrestled so part of my job was to remind Bud that Dan was fine and this was all a performance.

Once in Burlington, Bud just about hit the bleachers to save Dan from a crowd of frothing rednecks. I swear I had to grab the guy to calm him down. Looking back I should have let him go. Bud is a big guy and with Dan they could have cleaned house, then I could have a really cool story to tell.

We got to Lenoir and a crowd of about two hundred fifty were in attendance. At the Smoky Mountain shows the promotion would set up tables for the good guys to sell gimmicks and sign autographs before the matches began. At one of the tables was the Rock and Roll Express and I stopped by to say hello to Little Ricky Morton. Morton and I go way back, he was very friendly. As we talked, Robert Gibson wanted to know if we made him any signs. He had noticed the Tracy signs in the audience and he wanted a push.

I just looked at him and said, "Hell no! You guys are already over and Smothers needs some help!" Morton thought that was very funny but Gibson was pissed. Hey pal, I am working for the booker, not you.

I did have one Rock and Roll poster in my stack but I wasn't telling Ricky and Robert. After all the crap I gave those guys one simple sign would shock the hell out of them. This was going to be a ton of fun because it was a TV taping and every one of the big names in this promotion was going to rassle that night.

After three or four matches out walks Dan and his partner Robbie Eagle. (Yes, the guy that became The Maestro on WCW.) The ring announcer then told everyone that Dan is now, "John Hitchcock, from Parts Unknown!"

I just about lost a ball laughing at that one!

It turned out that Dan asked Jimmy Cornette if he could come out as John Hitchcock. Cornette looked at him and said, "From Parts Unknown!" They both thought it would be a blast to mess with me and I was quite honored.

And Eagle and Hitchcock's opponents were The Rock and Roll Express!

Ricky and Robert both walked to the ring and Ricky looked at me and said, "Is that your brother? I always wanted to kick your ass!"

The TV taping caught this whole moment perfectly. As the match began, you could see me holding a poster for the Rock and Roll. I am on the Front Row

cheering against myself!

But the really classic part of this was the TV announcers calling the match were Mid-Atlantic Legend Bob Caudle and Dutch Mantel. When 'John Hitchcock' lost the match to the dreaded Double Drop Kick, the match call was absolutely hysterical. Mantel said, "Well, a double Drop Kick may work on a John Hitchcock but I doubt it will work that well on the Moondogs!"

Hitchcock now an established jobber, then gets to taste a run in by those same Moondogs later in the show. And trust me, that coward Hitchcock took one shot from a stop sign and laid there like a dead fish.

But to be truthfully honest would any one expect any more effort from a bum like me?

I found out later that the other guy in the ring carrying Hitchcock volunteered to take the vacuum cleaner shot from the Moondogs so maybe Hitchcock was a little smarter than I thought. This match was very, very brutal, I was glad that the Bizarro World Hitchcock was in the ring instead of me.

Please do not ask me how I got Stan Lane's wrestling trunks.

The Cruise World Order Starts!

After watching wrestling on television and in person for over forty-five years, it was inevitable that I would climb into the ring.

That last statement is a total lie.

I was now in my forties, 'not in shape' is a kind description of me physically, I recently had a kidney transplant and could be back on dialysis with one bad fall from the ring. And let me make this perfectly clear, I have never been trained to do anything remotely like professional wrestling. So I never thought I would get closer to the ring than the somewhat safe front row.

That all changed when one person talked me into it. That person that really needs to sit on a shrinks couch is Chris Cruise. Cruise was for many years an announcer for WCW and knew a lot of people. Not people that I would want to know but that's another story.

Chris was very good friends with a local promoter, Chris Plano. Plano to his credit had purchased a small local promotion from an old wrestler named Ken Spence.

Spence seemed to always find a money mark to sell his promotion to. The thing would fall a part in a few months and he would sell it again to some other mark. Only, Chris Plano really worked his tail off and this small house of cards began to make a little money. This promotion started drawing about two to three hundred people a show!

Plano was a big fan of Cruise and he wanted him to join the promotion as a manager. Thinking back on it, having a guy with that much face time on television is a very good idea and it could help sell tickets. So this is where I got involved. Cruise wanted me to be in the ring with him so if any fan snapped and got in the ring; he could push me in front of them and get away. Cruise knew I could talk a lot of shit after sitting with me at all these independent shows. So I agreed to go along with this bit of nonsense.

Now, I needed a long stay on a shrink's couch too.

It all started in Burlington at a show in the armory. Ric Link was walking to the ring and he turned and saw Cruise and I sitting on the front row. Link went after Cruise but Cruise was way too quick for him to catch. But I was stupid and slow and he caught me cold. For a guy that weighs about 475 Link is very quick in short bursts. The outside ring barrier was made out of very cheap plastic plumbing pipes duck taped together. Link knocked me off my chair and hit me with all this stuff. And then put the boots to me. I had to lie there like a dead horse selling the hell out of it.

I mean, what could I really do but sell it?

And that was a very smart thing to do because it put Link over as a real killer heel. Of course, I looked like the innocent victim. The referee Dave Routh went down to the ring side and checked on me. Dave was a customer of mine at my comic book store, I guess he wanted a bigger discount so he took care of me, helping me to my feet after the match.

I acted as if I had been knocked unconscious and just now came to. I rose up to yell for justice, swinging my arms, punching the air wildly, threatening everyone involved that I'd press charges.

Maybe Plano saw all this and convinced him to let me bodyguard for Cruise? Maybe it was my personal charisma? Maybe Cruise really wanted me because of my fantastic bumping ability?

Or maybe it was the fact I agreed to work for free?

The locals really got into this and one guy said he knew a lawyer if I needed one. A friend of mine Doug Hilton was with us at this show and thought it was very funny only it was not a planned spot. Link just wanted to get some cheap heat at our expense.

So the groundwork for the Cruise World Order was ready for its next big step..

It's Show Time!

When the big night came I was very anxious to climb into the ring and start my wrestling career.

That's a total lie.

The day had finally arrived and I had no idea whether I really was going through with it. It only came together after Chris Cruise and I showed up at the Thomasville Armory. Cruise went back to the dressing room and worked out the whole procedure. I sat out in the crowd with Bruce and Big Eddie thinking that I could light up the Lumbee Warrior, if worse came to worse. The rest of the guys had no idea what was going on.

And I told nothing to no one. Hell, I didn't know anything.

I got the wave from Cruise and went back to discover just what was the deal. Cruise had gotten everything worked out with Chris Plano the promoter. We were going to stir up the crowd for three matches and then hit the ring.

It worked out much better than anyone could have dreamed.

We sat out front stirring up the crowd, being total assholes as usual, cheering for the Heels and hammering the Faces. Same old stuff, this crowd was used to this and most of them hated our group anyway so it came as quite a shock when things started happening. After the first match it was announced by Chris Plano that Rick Link was injured and could not make the program that night.

We all flew into a rage complaining about the promotion using the old bait and switch, that we all deserved a refund now, this was false advertising. Plano kind of blew us off and continued with the show while Cruise and I continued to bitch and moan about the whole deal.

Following the third match, Plano again announced again that Link wasn't going to wrestle that night. Cruise and I exploded again giving Plano hell that his promotion really sucked.

Plano then turned and told us that if we weren't happy we could get into the ring and do something about it. Cruise and I stood, giving the idea some deep thought as the crowd gave us shit about being chicken. So we both stepped on to the canvas, the first time I ever had been in a real ring. I went in under the first rope and almost busted my ass. A few fans in the crowd noticed that I screwed up and heckled me. It didn't bother me at all but you can bet that the next time I was going thru the second rope.

Plano immediately began insulting Cruise, claiming that he had no right telling him anything, referring to me as his stooge. Cruise calmly took the microphone and blew Plano out while I clotheslined the shit out of Plano from behind. The arena burst open with rage and excitement. It was really amazing to be in the ring and have all these fans go from shock to hate in fifteen seconds.

Plano left ringside very quickly so I grabbed up the mic from Cruise and began to give the security hell for being such slackers for not doing their jobs correctly. Then I explained to the crowd that they could feel honored to be in the presence of a man like Chris Cruise.

That really got the heat from these toothless wonders. From the ring announcer's table old time wrestling promoter Ken Spence called me out as a mark.

Me? A mark?

He was right but I was not going to back down to anyone at this point, I informed him that I knew all about Spence and his so-called career, ranting about him being trained, along with Rick Link, by the great Johnny Hunter, "Johnny Hunter was a great man and truly loved wrestling but he was not a great business man. And that there were many nights that Johnny didn't make enough money to pay the wrestlers so he paid them with day old donuts from his bread truck. And now, looking you Spence, I can tell who ate most of the cream filled! "

Spence weighed in at about 600 pounds. He was a beloved local legend, a perfect opportunity to establish that we were the bad guys. Then Cruise began railing about Link being a coward and a no talent for not showing up for the show.

Just then the houselights went out and Link walked slowly from the back to the ring. He had surgery legit on his arm but nobody knew he was there. Funny as we stood in the ring I realized that Cruise and I were going to be standing right next to Link when the lights came on and that was not going to be the right direction for our bit.

I grabbed Cruise, pulled him to the other side of the ring so that when the lights came back up we were both staring straight into the crowd and, man, I will never as long as I live forget the look of astonishment on those fan's faces. They all began to yell and point warnings that Link was just behind us.

We ignored them and resumed our trash talking about Link and the place got hotter. I turned to see Link first and hammed in up by walking over to Cruise to let him know Link was behind him in the ring and was pissed off.

We both grovelled, explaining to Link that we were just kidding around and he knew we were his biggest fans. The crowd turned on us then. Link seized the microphone to light into us, he even called me a "pussy." Link also said Cruise got his job blowing Eric Bishoff. Wow. I never knew that.

Link started to move towards Cruise, I stepped in to slow him down. I told Link if he took another step, I would have to kick his ass. Link threw one punch and I went down "fast as the sun". (A direct quote from Bruce Mitchell's column in The Torch.)

Just as Link closed in on the Cruiser, the place went dark again. When the lights came back on a hoard of wrestlers descended on the ring and assaulted Link, he was bleeding pretty badly. Cruise told everyone that next time we meet, Link is going to lose the Brass Knuckles Title.

Cruise and I fought our way back to the dressing room. Later that night, Bruce and I talked for hours about the whole experience at Denny's.

.

Karaoke Wrestling Federation - When your friends begin to promote indy shows

By Bruce Mitchell, Torch columnist;
from PWTorch.com 6-27-98

"We were somewhere around Barstow on the edge of the desert when the drugs began to take hold. I remember saying something like, 'I feel a bit lightheaded; maybe you should drive...' And suddenly there was a terrible roar all around us and the sky was full of what looked like huge bats..."

—Hunter S. Thompson, "Fear and Loathing in Las Vegas."

The following story is true. The names have not been changed. None of these people are innocent.

So I'm sitting on the couch on Friday afternoon when the phone rings.

"Wanna go to Thomasville?"

There's only one reason to go to Thomasville, N.C., a small town thirty miles or so west of Greensboro, N.C. It's not to see the world famous Big Chair that sits in the middle of what passes for downtown.

Although the Big Chair is quite a sight, since the thing is exactly what the name implies: a three story chair sitting in the middle of the town square, celebrating Thomasville's self-proclaimed status as the capital of the handmade furniture industry. Legend has it that late on certain balmy nights young Thomasvillians consummate their relationships on the huge chair cushion, but that could just be an ugly rumor.

No, the only reason to visit the peaceful community of Thomasville, for my friends at least, is to attend the New Dimension Wrestling shows at the National Guard Armory. New Dimension is another of the crop of independent promotions that have sprouted nationwide in wake of the Big Two's wrestling boom. The promotion is owned and run by Chris Plano, who doubles as the ring announcer.

In fact, Plano physically resembles nothing so much as what would happen if WCW ring announcers David Penzer and Gary Capetta, in the words of Conan O'Brien, Made It.

Needless to say, Plano is the only guy at these Armory shows dressed in a tuxedo. If our nation's last defense against the Nameless Hordes are the National Guard Armories in the Carolinas, with their peeling paint, bent rims, and lack of ventilation (not to mention a conspicuous lack of guns), it's going to be a short war. These fading relics of the '50s are just about perfect for indy wrestling: inexpensive to rent, easy to fill – maybe three hundred fans maximum, atrocious acoustics so it's easy to make a racket, and plenty of card tables for those cheapie merchandise vendors so the Gravedigger (Your Favorite Wrestler, it says on the table banner) can one day sell someone his picture.

The fans are great, too – an eclectic mix of the last few dozen fans who think It's Real, a few ECW Arena wannabes, little girls with crushes on Mr. Excellent and the Lumbee Warrior, and confused folks who wandered in looking for Stone Cold.

To his credit, for an independent promoter, Plano runs a pretty straight business. New Dimension throws a lot of shows in conjunction with minor league baseball games and county fairs in North Carolina, Virginia, and West Virginia—shows that make money because Plano usually sticks to a talent budget.

New Dimension shows follow the same formula, four or five matches featuring local indy "talent," a ref who turns heel early on but by the end of the night is back to face, a women's match, a match or two featuring juiced up green Power Plant guys who haven't yet jobbed on WCW Saturday Night, a main event featuring a Who's Was of pro wrestling with the likes of Pez Whatley, Ricky Morton, Bobby Fulton, or the 57 year old Jimmy Valiant, followed by one of those "Abandon Ship" Battle Royals to end the evening.

Usually it takes me about three months or so to forget the headache I get by the time I finish watching the World's Oldest Teenager Ricky Morton put on the same match for the 567th time and start getting sentimental for the "ambiance" of indy wrestling.

Unfortunately, it had only been about a month since my last New Dimension extravaganza and, well, I wasn't in the mood.

Until John Hitchcock, whom I've been watching wrestling with since the late '40s (well, it seems like it) said "Cruise is going to do an angle."

That got my attention.

"Cruise" is former WCW C-team play-by-play man Chris Cruise, who lives right outside of Greensboro, in Kernersville. Cruise holds the distinction of being the first and only announcer in WCW whose contract was not renewed during the Eric Bischoff administration, most likely because Bischoff wasn't a fan of Cruise's hammy style, something he had adopted with the encouragement of Dusty Rhodes, Larry Zbyszko, and Kevin Sullivan. Cruise, a mortgage banker by trade, had long held aspirations of running his own independent promotion and had become a fixture in the crowd at New Dimension shows.

Chris Cruise is not your average mortgage broker. When a local business weekly decided to do a profile on the mortgage man with the unusual second job, Cruise posed with his Japanese masks and regaled them with his views on the legalization of drugs and his plans to one day become a priest even though he wasn't sure about the celibacy thing (which was no surprise to anyone who knew him as one of the most relentless leg men around).

Cruise's behavior at these indy shows was hardly that of the typical Big Two wrestling "Suit," either. He sat right up in the front row and while he loudly protested whenever I frequently announced "WCW talent scout Chris Cruise is here tonight" to the wrestlers, he participated enthusiastically in the razzing of the local talent. Listening to Cruise invite fans who recognized him to go on mythical WCW tours to Bermuda with him and visit at the WCW offices was always an entertaining addition to the evening.

Inevitably, some wrestler was going to try to make Cruise part of his act. Enter the Beastmaster Rick Link.

Link was the local indy scene's version of Hulk Hogan, the most experienced hand in the locker room and the wrestler who protects his spot as the local legend with a fierce passion. Link, a native of nearby Lexington, has been kicking around the wrestling business for two decades, mostly in the southern territories and the dying days of Bob Geigel's Kansas City promotion, along with some tours of New Zealand – under names besides his own like KGB, 666, or The Beastmaster in a Kevin Sullivan-Dungeon of Doom type gimmick. Somewhere along the way he made a claim to the World's Brass Knuckles Championship.

Link is also the answer to a decent trivia question: Who was the last wrestler ever managed by the late Andy Kaufman? Link actually got to win the Southern title from Jerry Lawler during a short Memphis stint while managed by Jimmy Hart. Link's last bit of attention came in his hometown when he ran for Mayor of Lexington in 1997 as a publicity stunt and came in third. He's about six feet tall, bald, close to four hundred pounds, a throwback to the days when wrestlers were known for big beer bellies instead of acned backs. Link is old school enough to have gotten really pissed when he heard I explained blading on the radio one night.

Most Link matches go something like this: Link storms to the ring with gritted teeth, slugs and stomps his hapless opponent, slices his own head open with a razor, sells absolutely nothing, throws the guy out of the ring, smacks him with a chair with – depending on whether he has heat with the guy or not – a varying amount of force, they brawl around the ring for a couple of minutes, then he throws his foe back into the ring and pins him. The whole thing lasts ten minutes, tops.

Link is like New Jack and the Dudleys in that when he goes into the crowd, it's a good idea to keep your distance.

And pity the sap so naive he lets Link gig him with that blade. Forget Tommy Rich. The most blood I ever saw in a wrestling match, with the notable exception of Hiroshi Hase, was the night Link ripped the forehead off a poor ref. The stuff poured out like a faucet in puddles on the mat. The ref, who wanted to bleed just once, found himself semi-conscious on the mat. He was back at the next show, of course.

Link had made a habit of cussing out Chris Cruise after his matches, knowing that Cruise was such a hambone he'd throw a fit back at him.

So when Hitch told me Cruise was "going to do something" at the show, I wasn't surprised. I knew I wanted to see it. So it's off to T'ville to waste a perfectly good Friday night.

When we got there, seats were reserved for us on the second row aisle. I figured all Link was going to do was grab Cruise and smack him around after the match. I planned my escape route early.

After getting hit up ("Hey, Brother") at the door for a two dollar Jimmy Valiant bumper sticker by the freakish WWF Hall of Famer, watching an awful six-man tag with some guys who wanted to be wrestlers but not enough to actually work out or anything (the promotion's "wrestling school" is an abandoned house with no roof, by the way) and pleading with the stone-faced stripper-type valet to "change your expression" in the second match, the real fun began.

Chris Plano, in the tradition of American wrestling promoters everywhere (except Paul Heyman), always made sure to give himself plenty of time on the mic between matches. He gets into the ring to announce that Rick Link would not be on the show because of recent shoulder surgery. Cruise and Hitch both started yelling "ripoff" at Plano.

Then it got weird. To my utter shock, Cruise and Hitch stand up, walk up the ring steps, and get into the ring. Hitch throws a clothesline to the back of the diminutive Plano's head, grabbing the mic and starting babbling about the "Greatest Announcer of All Time, Mr. Cruise," and how he was "Mr. Cruise's Bodyguard, so show some respect" and then proceeded to blow out every member of the rapidly furious crowd while Cruise hopped around the ring taunting fans like Jimmy Hart on crystal meth.

The two got over huge. Hitch was spewing out decades of watching the likes of Jim Cornette and Terry Funk when he should have been having a life, while Cruise was finally shedding the straight jacket of his straight role. The fans were rabid. It was like seeing that slug sitting at the end of your couch watching Nitro step into the TV to join NWO Wolfpack.

It got even better. The fat, old wrestler on the sound board, Ken Spence, saw how big the two were getting over and wanted in on it, so he got on his mic and told Hitch, "Shut up, mark!"

Hitch: "Hey, Fat Boy, you don't want any of me or I'll tell everyone how when you used to work for (the late promoter) Johnny Hunter, he paid you in Day Ole Doughnuts, you Fatass."

A true story that brought the house down in the back room.

(By the way, exactly how fat is Ken Spence, who claims to, and may actually have for all I know, worked as one of the Assassins in Florida, and who had the single worst performance I ever saw in a main event when he rolled his girth into the ring against Rick Link last year? Well, the story goes, last summer the promotion used Spence on one side of a forklift to keep the wrestling ring balanced on the other side out at a ballpark. Unfortunately, everything tipped over, Spence was injured, and his wrestling career was over.)

Later that night the two heels are back in the ring, the lights go out, come back on, and there's Rick Link, who asks Cruise if he's still "sucking off Bischoff" (I guess not, his contract wasn't renewed). I start yelling at Link to kick Hitch in the kidney since he's only got one.

Sure enough, Hitch takes a bump from a Link punch. The sun goes down faster. Lights go out again, then come back on. Cruise's minions have supposedly jumped Link who is of course bleeding a gusher in the corner.

Now it was on.

Later shows featured the following: Link's brother-in-law hitting the ring on Cruise and Hitch because Link neglected to smarten him up and referee Dave Routh making the save in true Pee Wee Anderson fashion. Cruise throwing Macaroni to the "malnourished" T'ville fans. Hitch'n'Cruise "leading" Kimala II to the Brass Knucks Title one night, and losing it the next. Cruise being such a mark for himself that he has to be pulled away from calling a few kids "Little Bastards" while leaving the high school gym. Hitch bombing brutally in his hometown debut (Heh, Heh). Cruise asking to get shot with something else when he shoots the fans at the Armory with a Super

Soaker. The Iron Sheik yelling "He's foocking up my gimmick!" when Cruise tries to pick up a girl in the midst of a heel rant. ("You're all fat pigs. Well, except for you, baby.") Hitch telling me after I described on the radio how he screwed up taking the Camel Clutch, "I didn't screw up. I broke the hold. Get it right."

Take it from me, there's a lesson here. If any of your fanboy friends get a chance to break into the biz, do whatever you have to to stop them. If not you'll get to hear every inane booking idea that they or any of their pals come up with ("Let's call Link 'Hot Dog Man'") to the point that Nitro starts to make sense to you. You'll suffer through other jealous fanboys scheming to get in on the fun ("I'll drive up from Florida and bleach my hair blonde if you'll let me be your bodyguard, Hitch.") You'll hear gossip about indy wrestlers their mothers wouldn't be interested in. They'll be a central figure in a huge lawsuit filed by Titan Sports. (Wait, wrong fanboy...)

In the old days anyone wanting to get into pro wrestling got their leg broken by Verne Gagne or Bill Watts. Maybe they had a point, after all.

Bruce Mitchell of Greensboro, N.C. has been a Torch columnist since September 1990.

CHAIRSHOTS

ISSUE #16   DEC. 15, 1993 $3.00

John Hitchcock 93

To Virginia and the Brass Knuckles Title

After our first card, it was time for Hitchcock and Cruise to hit the road. This was rare in that we were booked to wrestle somewhere in Virginia. I can't remember exactly where but it was another youth center type place right near the North Carolina border.

I wasn't going to drive very far for no pay but Chris Cruise really wanted to go. After we rolled into Virginia, we stopped at a real dive for a Diet Pepsi. This place was an honest to God hellhole of a store and it made quite an impression on both of us. There was very little for sale except warm drinks and oatmeal cookies. They also had an extra room built on the side of the building for people to scratch off their lotto tickets. It had four cheap card tables and a few folding chairs, the floor was covered in lotto ticket scrapings.

When I walked into this cinder block room, I could hear crunching. I ain't kidding, this was one of the saddest places I have ever seen in my life outside of a wrestling arena.

Cruise and I got the hell out of there and proceeded to the show.

There was a good turn out waiting, maybe two hundred twenty five paid. It was very interesting because I got my first taste of wrestling promoter paranoia. Cruise and I both figured that we would do the same thing we did the last show. It made sense because it worked so well and it got us both over as assholes with the crowd, Chris Plano and Rick Link said that we couldn't do that because of the internet.

I couldn't believe it. Who cares about the internet?

We had to come up with something quick so I made something up. Cruise never had one idea himself, he would just tell me to do it.

We entered the ring alone and told the assembled that, "Last week we kicked Rick Link's ass and he isn't going to ever wrestle again. We now own this town and all you rednecks will have to live with that fact." I looked over at Plano sitting at ringside with a redhead and I harassed her for being country. This girl, it turned out, was one of Link's ring rats and she sold all this heckling well. Trust me folks, when Chris Cruise starts giving fans heat, it ain't very pretty.

After that, we left the ring claiming there wasn't anyone tough enough to deal with the Cruise World Order. We really couldn't walk back to the back room, so we just walked outside to the back parking lot. I swear we didn't know where we were going, we just went. The next match was Link versus some jobber and he killed the poor guy in about two minutes. Then Link yelled for us to come out and talk that trash to his face.

We both strolled out to the ring while the fans were really giving us shit. It worked! Somehow I was ordered by Cruise to get in the ring and face Link. Why I did that remains a mystery because I usually am not that stupid.

I went to the center and assumed the Karate Kid crane pose before Link knocked me out with one punch. I took a slow bump out of the ring and on to the floor. I sold it like I was near death. Referee Dave Routh ran down to check on me, asked if I was okay and that his wife was worried about me. I said I was fine and Dave called me an asshole.

As I lay there a woman on the front row walked over to me with these warm words of encouragement, "Get up you dumb ass!" Cruise threatened to fight Link but we instead ran out of that place and headed back to Greensboro laughing all the way home.

And we did not stop at that cinder block hellhole on the way home.

Score card:
Cruise $50.00
Hitchcock zip.

Back to Thomasville and The Title

Both Chris Cruise and I knew this show would make or break us with this wrestling group, we were both determined to put on a memorable performance.

We got to the Thomasville Armory about an hour early to hash out the details with promoter Chris Plano. Plano loved our ideas and, from that match on, we just did what we wanted to in the ring.

This is what happened. I walked in the front door and purchased a ticket. This showed the fans I was not part of the show. And I had my arm in a sling selling the injury from last week's beat down. It was a pitiful sight.

I was sitting on the Front Row with Bruce and Big Eddie and all the fans were giving me hell for being such a wussy. I sold that injury like crazy throughout three matches. When Plano took to the ring I began berating him, wondering out loud if this promotion had casualty insurance because I wasn't a wrestler and I was seriously injured.

Plano then asked me up to the ring to confirm there was an injury. Funny thing about Chris Plano is that he really did hate it when I called New Dimension Wrestling, "New Dumb Wrestling" He got angry every damn time!

Anyway, as Plano turned his back, I clotheslined him, then removed my arm from the sling and told all the rednecks that I fooled them all! That is one of the oldest tricks in the book. Then I introduced the man with the money, the great Chris Cruise! Cruise walked out with an arm load of my posters and the heat began to rise.

We both were in the ring railing against the fans for thinking that we had ever quit the business. We were here to run that fat ass Beast Master Rick Link out of the New Dimension Wrestling forever. Then we asked Link to come to the ring because we had a special gift for him. Link walked to the ring acting really pissed. (Maybe he was.)

I informed him my Uncle Ted didn't like him using the name Beast Master because Turner Classics copyrighted it. It was against the law for him to use the name so we came up with a new one just for him.
I unrolled a poster with a cartoon drawing of Link dressed as an Oscar Mayer

Hotdog with a toilet plunger on his head. "See now you can be Corn Dog Rick Link! Then, at intermission, you can make an extra buck selling hotdogs to the marks! It is in your best interest to do this or I'll see to it Ted Turner will sue you!" I was on a roll.

Link stared at both of us and asked if we thought this was somehow funny. Of course we did, that was a stupid question. Link then laughed that Cruise got his job with WCW by kissing Eric Bischoff's ass. That may have been true but that was a rude thing to bring up at this time so I threaten to kick Link's ass.

Now remember that Link is about 450 pounds, dressed in black, his head looks like a road map, and he had the reputation of beating the hell out of everybody he had ever been in the ring with. Link hit me with one punch and I sold it like a rifle shot in Dallas. Just as Link closed in on the begging-for-mercy Cruise, the Ugandan Giant Kamala Two ran out to the ring with a coat hanger, attacking Link with it and really chopped the hell out of him.

The coat hanger was a brilliant special effect because it did look bad for Link. Link juiced and all hell broke loose from the crowd. Cruise, being such a fine gentleman, began laying the boots to Link and I started choking him. Hey, I wanted to get in on the fun too.

It was an amazing display of violence after which we beat a hasty retreat to the back room. The fans were throwing cups and plastic bottles at us but when you're behind a 450-pound Ugandan hauling ass, people get out of the way real fast.

When we finally got to the back room I realized that my hands and shirt were covered in Link's blood. It was ghastly and Cruise was covered too. About seven or eight minutes passed before Link was helped to the back room looking like he had been in a car wreck. We all talked it over and were thrilled with how things were going.

That's the odd thing about wrestling, you can stand there talking to a guy covered in his own blood and it's no big deal.

About an hour later we all walked out to the ring and demanded the Brass Knuckles Title. Our reasoning being that, after that beating Link took there was no possible way he could defend the title.

The lights were down real low as I was celebrating the future championship when Link ran in the front door of the Armory and jumped all over me!

He jerked me off the second rope and I took a hard fall. I sold it like death, careening outside the ring to the floor.

The match began with Link kicking the shit out of Kamala. Cruise ran out of the ring just in time. In my booking concept Cruise was the carrot on the stick that Link wanted but could never get. To this day I should have been the carrot because I always took the beating every damn night and I wasn't very good at it.

As the match went on Cruise threw some powder into Link's eyes and Kamala took the offensive. A chair was crushed on Links head and we got the one, two, three! Link hit another gusher and we were the new Brass Knuckle Champs. Cruise ran over to me on the floor, I looked at him and asked, "Did we win?"

Cruise laughed but the crowd heat was growing. When Kamala rolled out of the ring with the Title I grabbed the belt and held it over our heads bragging, "We are your champions!" That's when a green bottle was hurled at us that hit Kamala right on his forehead. Thank God it was plastic.

Kamala looked over at me, "I am out of here brother!" I replied, "I am with you brother!"

I turned to see Cruise kicking Link who was slumped in the far corner. An EMT attendant was trying to help Link so Cruise slapped the guy's hat off his head. This guy got really hot and dived at Cruise. The referee Dave Routh threw a pretty tackle on the guy and Cruise was able to follow us to the back.

Dave Routh saved Cruise's life that night. Audience members were losing it at this point with popcorn, hotdogs, and drinks flying at us in all directions as we got the hell out of the way.

We didn't realize at the time that Link had defended that belt for years without a defeat and the fans went from shock to hatred very fast.

Once in the back room Cruise and I looked at each other and laughed and hugged each other. Over in the far corner there was the main event standing there waiting to go on. Jimmy 'The Boogie Woogie Man' Valiant had to follow that unrivaled pandemonium and was really steamed about it Sorry Dude, we got over, top that.

Fifteen minutes later Link was carried back to the back room and as soon as he got out of sight he broke in to the biggest smile I have ever seen. He was so happy and kept saying over and over, "Now that was some real heat!" We all shook hands and I felt like a million bucks.

I went over to Ben Peacock (Kamala's real name) to thank him for doing such a super job and this wonderful man asked, "Do you always get heat like that every night? That is the most heat I've seen in years! If it's anything like that tomorrow, I am not showing up." He was being serious too, this guy had just gotten back from a tour of Japan.

While the celebration was going on backstage a mentally disturbed individual and his girlfriend muscled their way in the dressing room door demanding retribution! It was the paramedic Cruise assaulted during the match who, it turns out, was Rick Link's future brother-in-law,. He was consumed with anger, pushing his way into the dressing room so one of the wrestlers stepped forward and told him to get lost.

Since I was Cruise's bodyguard I did the only smart thing and hid behind the weight lifting machine. This guy wouldn't take no for an answer and when he spotted Cruise he went after him. The wrestler at the door maneuvered the EMT out then threw a punch at him. The paramedic ducked just in time but his girlfriend didn't and took one to the chest that knocked her down. I began to wonder if I was going to make it home alive that night. Fortune smiled at us, Boogie was starting his match so all the attention switched over to that spectacle and we were able to get to our cars and get the hell out of there.

Needless to say, the heat that night would never be duplicated in Thomasville. Later Cruise, Bruce, and I got together at Shoney's to laugh about it for hours.

Score Card:
Cruise $80.00
Hitch: zip.

Page & The Burlington Death Match

The next day was the highly anticipated rematch with Kamala versus Link for the Brass Knuckles Title. This show was in Greensboro and was held at Page High School.

Page is a legendary school in Greensboro that I attended for one year. We were all informed that this show was going to be a sell out because it was a fund raiser for the school and all the boosters and students had been out selling tickets.

When Cruise and I arrived we could tell that nobody had sold a lot of tickets, we got the impression that Page was hoping this would just go away. But the show would go on!

The crowd was better than the parking lot led us to believe with about three hundred in attendance. But there was one huge problem. The fine folks at Page would not let any chairs on the basketball floor so there was no one around the ring to yell at. You only had people seated in the bleachers and that was like wrestling at an opera. The distance made it very difficult to get heat with the crowd but we tried our best to raise a little hell.

Cruise and I went to work on the crowd, it was quite a change but the fans there did get into our act. Cruise could never get enough of yelling at the children in attendance. I believe he must have been a frustrated teacher at one time because he would scream at any toddler for hours to get some heat. There were a bunch of fans there from Thomasville and a few friends of mine from my comic store, Parts Unknown at the show.

These wise asses decided to turn on us that night, I can still remember such thrilling signs as, "Flush The John "and "Cruise really does suck" flashing from the crowd at us. We felt the love that night.

The show was uneventful except for a few staining memories. We were in the main event that night but the show dragged on for about four hours before we got to our match. Man, was it boring sitting back in the locker room waiting and waiting to do something.

One thing that did happen a lot was Pez Whatley walking around nude without a care in the world. Now I know why he was called the pistol man. Another thing that was interesting was watching Kamala Two put on his headhunter face paint. He was very methodical doing this, it took him about fifteen minutes. I told you it was boring back there.

Another thing that was strange, I began to notice how so many of the wrestlers walked around acting like they were the toughest guy in the room. Funny, the toughest guys never had to do shit to prove it, most knew it and accepted it for a fact.

For example, I was in the locker room once with the Masked Super Star and he was the calmest most pleasant guy I ever talked to, much more concerned with his business at the time and thanked me for letting him use my phone. I was totally messed up talking to him in his wrestling gear, I had all these Buzz Sawyer flashbacks so I just kept on marking out for him.

The guys who were strutting around talking the most shit felt they needed to re-enforce their rank and status, for whatever reason. I never understood all that macho bullshit, but then again I was a mark pussy what did I really know about the back room pecking order?

When it was time for the main event we lost the title back to Link in about seven minutes. That was a huge mistake.

We should have kept the title and had Link chase us around for six months... but Link was the booker so he got the belt back. After the match I was supposed to help Kamala clear his eyes from the power Cruise accidentally tossed in his eyes. Suddenly Kamala stood up but I was kind of leaning on his back when he did this. I was thrown halfway across the ring on my head.

This is not a good thing to have happen, trust me. After the show Bruce and I had to physically drag Chris Cruise away from a bunch of kids that he was screaming at. I never used bad language in the ring but Cruise cursed like a drunken sailor. Those kids got their money's worth that night, that's for sure.

Scorecard:
Cruise $110.00
Hitch, zip.

Our next show was in the Burlington Armory, the place was steaming with heat. We were lucky that night, Cruise and I got to manage Ricky Nelson. In my opinion Nelson was the finest wrestler in the NDW and deserved to be in the WCW or WWE based on talent and ability alone. He really could do anything in the ring. Nelson had one major flaw that prevented us staying together longer as a team. He could talk trash very well and really didn't need us so we only worked with him for a few matches.

That night we had a ball stirring up the crowd, about three minutes into the match Nelson called us over to him, saying something about avoiding the right side of the crowd. Cruise got the scoop—someone in the crowd was brandishing a pistol at Nelson! Needless to say the match ended quickly and Nelson, Cruise, and I hauled ass back to the dressing room.

We all were scared something could go terribly wrong. Anyway before the next match Link grabbed Bruce Mitchell on the Front Row and managed to tear apart his T-shirt. Link thought this was really funny and expected Bruce to write him up in The Pro Wrestling Torch out of anger.

Bruce was pissed but he never granted Link his wish.

After our match ended I slipped out the back door to go to my car when I heard a drunken voice yelling in my direction. Standing behind me, getting into his vehicle, was a black guy and his drunken girlfriend. The girl screamed in a screeching voice, "There is one of those motherfuckers!"

The guy reached into his coat and pulled out a pistol and demanded that I tell Nelson and Cruise, the next time he saw them, that he was going to get them. I readily agreed with this madman and told him I would gladly do so.

What was I suppose to do? The two lunatics finally got in their car and drove off. I was really shook up and got back to my car as fast as I could where Bruce was waiting with his torn shirt, giving me grief.

I told him, 'Shut up and get in the car!' but that just pushed Bruce's buttons and he began to really give me shit. I looked him right in the eyes and explained that a nut over there just pulled a gun on me. That did the trick. Bruce jumped in the car and we drove like hell back to Greensboro.

Scoreboard:
Cruise $150
Hitch, soiled pants

A gift from writer/editor Archie Goodwin.

Referee Time at the Warthogs

This story takes us to Winston- Salem, North Carolina where I was supposed to be Cruise's bodyguard but the referee was a no show. There I was, the hated 'Enforcer,' being talked into refereeing by one of the Fantastics, Bobby Fulton. I have a lot of respect for Fulton. He was one of the few guys in New Dimension Wrestling that really knew what he was doing. I always felt safe in the ring with him... that would soon change.

Anyway, Bobby was really hammering at me to be the night's ref but I didn't want any part of that. But he wouldn't let up. I remember Bobby looking at me and saying, "Come on John, How many years have you watched wrestling? Thirty? I think you can figure it out. There is nothing to it! Just count the pins. NO BIG DEAL!" And the classic guilt line of all time, "We need you."

So like the fool I am, I agreed to do it. After all it was easy right? But there was a huge problem. Huge being my fat ass and the problem being the ref shirt was a medium. I swear to god I looked like a stuffed sausage in that damn shirt and sadly I knew it and I still found myself walking to the ring. What a dummy. So the first match was two young guys in a singles. I swear those guys did everything they knew in three minutes and the match was supposed to go fifteen. And I didn't think about telling them to slow down and I was dying in about sixty-three seconds.

Those guys had me jumping up and down every ten seconds. I finally started using the famous Broncho Lubich one knee pin count. I hated that stuff in World Class but what is a guy suppose to do when he is dying up there. Make no mistake about it, it was hot as hell in the ring.

Then I blew out my hamstring. Where was Tommy Young when you need him? The next match was a midget match. And I just about quit because you have to get low for those guys. I looked over at Cruise and Fulton and they were laughing their ass off at me. Welcome to the little leagues pal.

Thank God the last match was the main event. Scrappy? Scrappy? I need a tag. The match was Fulton with Chris Cruise as his evil manager versus The Beast Master, Ric Link. Cruise got lost early in the match, it was the first time I wasn't directing traffic. Cruise was supposed to interfere but he kept missing his spots and that drove both Fulton and Link crazy. The one thing you do not want to face is an angry Beast Master. Or Fulton for that matter. This match was to have a ref bump in it but I didn't know when the damn thing was coming, until Fulton called for it out of nowhere.

Suddenly, Fulton said, "Mister Referee, it is time for your bump." I was standing in the middle of the ring and was not ready for this at all. Fulton came off the ropes and knocked the wind out of me. I went head over heels in a 540 and landed on my head against the ropes. I was seeing stars big time and was convinced I had broken my leg. I was just knocked silly, luckily nothing was fractured. They went for the finish with Link winning the match and I was supposed to count the three count. It took me a while to crawl over there and make the one two three.

It was very dramatic because the crowd really did wonder if I could make it or not. The bump was that bad. I crawled over on my elbows and hit the count and the place got a huge pop but I was dying. I took my time getting to the back of the baseball field, Chris Plano was nowhere to be found.

Yep, the promoter had disappeared. I was going to get paid for this or I was going to kill the guy. I was really hurting but I was hot enough to do real damage to Plano.

I finally found him and my payoff was twenty dollars. Twenty dollars was a shitty payoff but it did mean something to me. I was now a paid professional. We did return to Winston Salem where I got to manage with Cruise, we delivered some real heat. Cruise was really good playing a heel, the crowd despised him. I fed him a line about the Demon Deacons sucking at football. Which was true. But Cruise didn't follow sports so he dumped all over NC State instead. That is a face move in Winston Salem.

Anyway, I began to pick up the heel slack and began hammering Wake Forest for not winning anything in sports period. I even brought up the fact that, even with Tim Duncan, they still didn't win shit. Proof that they suck. Wake ain't the Tar Heels, that's for sure. I really got those fans inflamed, I didn't know it but that night at the ballpark was a Wake Forest Homecoming, these folks were blistering hot. Hey, all I was doing was telling the truth.

As we left the ring the Winston Salem Warthog Mascot started talking trash to me. I couldn't believe it, even the guy in the stupid outfit wanted a piece of me! I bet it was funny to the crowd watching me throwing a stiff arm at this Warthog as he chased me down. That was a very bad move because mascot boy got some momentum behind him and tackled my ass in the outfield which really fucked me up. I had a huge knot on my leg, I didn't think I could make our next match.

But I had to go on because Cruise and I were managing a midget that night. I booked the whole match and got to choke the good guy midget and then get panned by Cruise to set up the pin. Think about it, how many times to you get to choke a midget in your life?

Your scorecard,
Cruise $300
Hitch, your humble servant, $40.

Show Time with the Bats

Yes, New Dimension Wrestling did do a few shows in Greensboro, most were held at the old War Memorial Stadium, a baseball field built just after World War II, the concrete was crumbling in some places. It can be seen in the movie Bull Durham. I watched my brother Sparky play football there as a kid and I loved going there for any reason.

It did have a creepy side to it. There were two large metal plaques outside honoring the local dead from WW2. One side was a listing of dead soldiers and the other side said Colored Dead.

Well, NDW did wrestle a lot of paid shows there, usually after the Bats baseball games. The crowd was a bunch of bored fans with nothing else to do but they usually numbered about four hundred for a good show and thirty-five for a slack one.

It was very odd to watch them move the ring from behind the outfield to the playing field using a huge crane like machine that was always out of balance, it really did mess up that ring. It was a death trap to wrestle in after all that moving.

Cruise and I were hanging around the concession stand when a guy walked up and asked if I was the referee at the Warthog game last week. I said yep, I was that guy. He then asked how did I learn to take such a great bump? Did I go to a special school to learn how to fall like that?

Chris Cruise stood there in total amazement, quiet as a tomb.

I just figured it was better to be honest with him. I told him that was the real deal. Bobby Fulton just crushed me and that was the first time I had ever been a referee. And it was going to be the last time too.

This guy told me he and his friends couldn't stop talking about it., that the bump stole the show.

I caught up with Bobby later that night and asked him why he decided to kill me. This will give you an insight to Fulton. Bobby said that Cruise was lost the whole night and was not in the right place so he was going to make sure this was going to look good.

"But Bobby, you knew I had never refereed and didn't know how to work"

Bobby, "Yeah, but it was the finish. It had to look good." Thanks a lot pal.

These shows were pretty effective and most of them had a young team named the Hardy Boys on the card. And Jeff was just as fearless then as he is now, he took some unbelievable bumps every match. Matt was solid and getting better all the time. We all knew that they could make the big time, if they lived that long.

We had another kind of famous person in this group. John 'Fairplay' Dalton of Survivor. The first time we used him he did a run in from the crowd totally drunk out of his mind. Fairplay was so scared he blew his spot, referee Dave Routh had to grab him so Cruise could give him a chair shot. I got to chair him too but I took pity and airballed it. Why I didn't spill his brains out right there and then remains a mystery to this day.

Oh, and there was the time Ric Link dropped the N bomb in front of a bunch of school kids. Now that was entertainment.

.

Flyin' Brian

They didn't call him the Loose Cannon for nothing.

On the few occasions I got to talk with Brian Pillman all of the conversations were memorable. The Night Of The Squeegee, he walked over to me after his match and asked me if I had an extra cardboard squeegee. He wanted it so I gave him one of my extras. Pillman then walked to the dressing room doing the tomahawk chop and laughing his ass off.

Later in Florida, I ran into him in a bar and asked what he did with that squeegee I gave him in Greensboro? He laughed out loud, grabbed me around the neck and said, "I carry it in my bag. I take it everywhere so if the big pussy Sid ever wants some, I'll kick his goddamn ass with it!"

You've got to love a guy with that kind of sense of humor. Flashback to a Winston-Salem WCW Nitro show. Those shows were live so anything could happen.

I wasn't Front Row as was customary, my seats were about five rows deep, nothing to sneeze at. It turned out those were the best seats in the house that night. During the show Brian Pillman unexpectedly ran out into the crowd, right into my section. Hell, the guy was right on top of me. Pillman had been 'fired' by WCW and he was not supposed to be at the show.

As he bolted into the crowd he was carrying a sign. that said, PILLMAN. COM or something like that. I knew it was staged and decided to have some fun with him. Nothing like giving the guy some needed heat. But man, he had that in bucket loads.

Anyway, I started yelling at him, giving him some shit. "Hey, Pillman! What are you doing here? You are supposed to be in ECW! You are trying to ruin our show?" (Our Show being the funniest thing I could think of.) Pillman then looked right me and cut loose with this gem. "Shut the hell up, fat ass! I'll go whereever I want to and nobody is going to stop me!"

For the record that was the first time anyone ever called me a fat ass. Truth hurts. Pillman then jumped up on my seat and started waving that sign around. There was one problem. He was wearing boots and they were way to slippery to stand on those cheap plastic chairs. He was falling all over the place trying to get up there. So I reached up and grabbed him by his belt to steady him. "I got ya brother." "Thanks Brother."

Pillman was able to get in camera range and attract all the attention he needed. As I was holding him up Pillman cut loose with some more curses at me then ran like hell when Bishoff and the WCW security showed up. "Thanks again brother." "No problem, brother."

That's the wrestling business.

.

Benoit

I went to a tribute show for the ailing referee Brian Hilderbrant put on by WCW and it was truly a heartfelt effort. Chris Cruise, Bruce Mitchell and I drove to Johnson City Tennessee, about four hours by car one-way. All of us knew Brian and wanted to show our support for him personally.

There were a ton of wrestlers, announcers, and friends there. And there were many stories to tell.

We all went around to the back of the building trying to get a pass in. Bruce told about five people that he was B-R-U-C-E, M-I-T-C-H-E-L-L and nobody seemed to care. We, of course, loved that and ribbed him all night about it. We finally all bought tickets, my idea, to a very packed, near sellout show.

There were a bunch of people in the wrestling business hanging out. Thanks to Mark Madden, he got me to the back and I had a great opportunity to talk to a lot of the finest wrestlers in the world that night.

There was The Brave: Brian Hilderbrant was very kind with his time and went out of his way to greet everyone. He was dying of cancer and everyone knew it but he was so brave that everyone felt good about him being there. Arn Anderson kidded Brian about needing attention so badly.

There was The Falling Star: Lex Luger, who wrestled that night and nobody even talked to him when he was leaving.

There was The Comic Relief: Cruise went up to Harlem Heat and joked that they were the most uncoordinated black men he ever met. Stevie Ray and Booker T laughed out loud at that line.

There was The Discarded: As I walked around the back stage I noticed a lone familiar figure. It was Pez Whatley an NWA fixture for over twenty years. Pez was now hired to put up and move the wrestling ring from town to town. Whatley should have been hired as a trainer in my opinion but he looked very lonely sitting by himself. I grabbed Cruise, "Hey, Is that the Pistol Man?"

Cruise said, "Yeah, I think it is! Pistol Pez, it's great to see you!" I told him,

"Man, what a legend!" You have never seen a bigger smile in your life.

And there were The Dreamers: The Main Event was Chris Jericho, Dean Malenko, Eddie Guerrero, and Chris Benoit in a big tag team match. All these incredible wrestlers were very short. I am six foot two and a half and they all barely cleared my shoulder. I was told not to talk to Malenko because he was the kind of guy that got into character and shouldn't be disturbed before his match. That was kind of sad because I wanted to tell him what a huge fan I was of his father, Boris.

Jericho was very friendly. It was shocking to notice just how young he looked. He had peach fuzz on his chin. And his boots had lifts on them that would have made Bettie Page blush.

Eddie had a quick smile and overflowed with personality. He was surprised that I even knew who he was. And he thanked me for taking the time to talk with him.

Last was Chris Benoit.

I walked over to him and told him I thought he was the best wrestler in the world. Benoit asked me what my name was and I told him. Benoit said, and I quote, "John, that is very flattering but remember, there is another guy in the ring helping me look good. Don't ever forget that."

I replied, "Yeah, I know, I know, but right now I think your matches are incredible. You are the man." Chris Benoit just smiled that toothless grin, shook my hand and said, "Just remember, the other guy making me look good."

His handshake was like a vise. And he too barely cleared my shoulder. It was like Benoit's hand was made out of a chain covered in burlap. The only other handshakes I ever experienced like that were from boxer Joe Frazier and football immortal Jim Brown.

Last weekend, Chris Benoit killed his wife Nancy, his son Daniel, and then himself. I really do not want to rehash any of the painful facts. There are many great artists that have done very bad things. But I still can enjoy their paintings. I hope that one day I can watch a great Chris Benoit match without thinking about the sad ending of his life.

Right now, I can't.

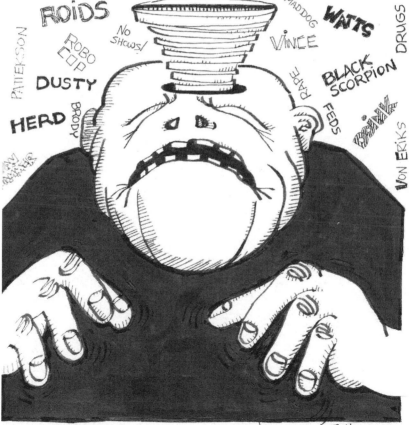

The Gravedigger and the White Boy

There are always bizarre moments when it comes to wrestling in the minor leagues but this one instance really does stand out. The New Dimension Wrestling group returned to Burlington for a show in the armory. Cruise and I were asked by the promoter to manage this guy called the Gravedigger. You sharp witted readers have probably guessed that this guy was an Undertaker rip-off. Well, you are right but he wasn't the sharpest marble in the drawer if you get my drift.

The Digger was trained by Rick Link and had been on these shows for a few years. It was strange because he was a very big guy, about 375lbs. In the world of the independents, that is a very big guy. But it was my impression that he didn't have a killer personality.

He was a nice guy that needed to break bad and kick some serious ass to get over but he never really was able to do that. The Gravedigger was really trying to get over. He had a gimmick table were he sold foam shovels to all his fans. At one show he juiced like crazy and after his match walked over to his table and bled all over his stuff and then sold them to the Little Diggers.

Cruise and I managed him that night and we really put him over. The fans went crazy when he joined the Cruise World Order but Cruise wasn't thrilled with the prospect of managing somebody we didn't really like. When we went back to the locker room the Digger thought he was the reason he got over and basically blew us off. That was not cool.

We decided to go a different path.

The next show the Cruiser went to Chris Plano, the promoter, and told him we wanted to manage a guy named The Dirty White Boy. Not The White Boy, Tony Anthony, but a person named Kerry who was a great guy and a super brawler when the situation called for it. We both wanted to prove to Digger that we were the cause of his heat, besides we really wanted to work with Kerry. Kerry claimed he once wrestled for Bill Watts at one time on the under card so that was enough for us.
The way the match was booked we were all in the ring when Cruise and I told the Digger he was out and White Boy was in. As soon as Cruise said that White Boy went off and crushed the poor guy. Crushed is not the

right adjective that I should use here. I think destroy with anger fits better.

White Boy jerked up Digger and plastered the guy all over the armory. It was unbelievable. The match was no DQ so it just went on and on with White Boy hitting Digger with anything that was not nailed down. There was a garbage can that was made during the depression and I bet it weighed forty-five pounds empty. White Boy picked that can up and folded it over Diggers head then put him through a heavy wooden door. One of those gymnasium doors that are about three inches thick. Why the Gravedigger didn't try selling any of this is still a great mystery to me personally.

Man, it was beautiful watching those guys basically kill each other for twenty bucks each. I finally went to the referee and yelled at him to call a count out. The ref just looked at me and said, "Are you crazy? I ain't stopping this! This match is fuckin' great!"

Can't argue with that logic. One of the fans ringside started giving me hell for trying to stop a fight my guy was winning. I told him I didn't want my meal ticket breaking his hands on that big goof, which kind of makes sense.

He was right but the match was totally out of hand so I went up the bell ringer and told him to ring the bell and stop the match.

I thought the referee was going to beat my ass for that but it was time to take it home before Digger ended up in the hospital eating soup for six weeks.

From then on the Dirty White Boy represented the Cruise World Order. And we both were very lucky to have him on our side.

Santa Claus is Coming to Town

There's really nothing like the world of small time independent wrestling. The strangest things happen all the time. Thing is, very few people stop and take notice.

One night in Burlington Chris Plano had a great idea. It was close to Christmas so he wanted a wrestler to dress up like Santa and give out candy to all the kids in attendance. But none of the guys on the card wanted to do this Santa deal. We were all involved with working out our match strategies and couldn't be bothered.

Turns out we all should have taken turns being Santa. Why you ask?

Well, Plano gave his Santa Claus suit to a homeless guy and had him give out the treats. Sounded like a solid plan. The guy worked cheap and he wanted to do it. There was one major problem that Plano did overlook. The homeless Santa smelled really, really bad.

How foul did Santa smell? Like he was rolled in cow manure for eight days, worked in a tobacco field for two months, then put on the suit. And I ain't kidding. The kids would run up to Santa, get a whiff, yell to their parents, "Mom! Dad! Santa smells bad!" and run off.

Imagine that, a kid that wouldn't take free candy from a walking asshole. It was so funny we almost died laughing in the back—until Santa walked back and we all smelled the funk from twenty feet away.

The funny thing is Santa didn't understand why the kids were repelled by him. It was amazing. And Plano never took steps to get that guy out of the suit... what an image NDW was casting now.

We even tried to run an angle with smelly Santa. Ricky Nelson tried to get him in the ring to clothesline him but Santa balked, leaving Nelson hanging in the wind. That angle would have brought the armory down. Cruise and I were in the back laughing so hard we almost fell over.

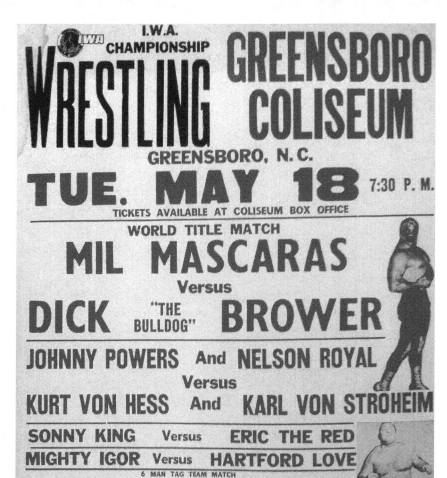

I.W.A. CHAMPIONSHIP WRESTLING

GREENSBORO COLISEUM

GREENSBORO, N. C.

TUE. MAY 18 7:30 P.M.

TICKETS AVAILABLE AT COLISEUM BOX OFFICE

WORLD TITLE MATCH

MIL MASCARAS

Versus

DICK "THE BULLDOG" BROWER

JOHNNY POWERS And NELSON ROYAL

Versus

KURT VON HESS And KARL VON STROHEIM

SONNY KING Versus ERIC THE RED

MIGHTY IGOR Versus HARTFORD LOVE

6 MAN TAG TEAM MATCH

BEAUTIFUL BRUCE And THE MAULERS

Versus

MAN MOUNTAIN WILLIAMS — NICK DE CARLO — ARGENTINE APOLLO

EL CONQUISTIDOR Vs LUIS MARTINEZ ★ PHIL WATSON Vs JOHNNY RINGO

The only time the AWA came to the Greensboro Coliseum.

A Black Cloud

New Dimension Wrestling was growing as the Cruise World Order began catching on. We started wrestling in front of about one hundred and fifty people and the crowd on most Saturday nights swelled to two hundred and fifty. The reason honestly was not just Cruise and I stirring the shit every night. The younger wrestlers began to really catch on to how to wrestle and work the crowd. And the crowd really began to turn out to see what was going on.

I mean, I would like to think it was all me but it wasn't.

One night a Black Cloud showed up out back of the armory. The Black Cloud was Manny Fernandez. You all know that Manny was a big deal with Jim Crockett Promotions tagging with Dusty Rhodes and Rick Rude but he really meant nothing without any publicity. And showing up demanding to wrestle at a high price to boot was not a good thing.

I will never forget the moment Manny walked in saying that Willie Clay told him to be here and work the show. Now I have never heard this guy Willie Clay but Fernandez was really stirring up trouble and make no doubt about it, he was a very intimating guy in person. Chris Plano folded like an old paper cup and put him on the ticket. But you couldn't blame him. Manny acted like he was going to kick his ass and he probably would have. That turned out to be the biggest mistake Plano ever made.

The locker room went from a bunch of fun guys to be around to a group that was stepping on eggshells every night. The oxygen was taken out of NDW and the promotion started to go downhill from that moment on.

Now that I am thinking about it, what was Manny's real name? He is definitely not the guy who played football for the Miami Dolphins. I found that guy's football card and they are not the same person. And the real Fernandez was a member of the famous No Name defense that went 17 and 0 for the Dolphins. That publicity made this "Manny" take his name and profit off of it.

This guy works everybody everywhere he goes. Personally, I fear the guy on many levels. At many shows he purposely hurt other wrestlers to increase his reputation as a bad ass. One match in High Point, he broke a fan's leg just for the fun of it.

Funny thing, Rick Link acted like Manny being there was a great thing and started hanging out with him. It was very odd to watch since Manny was taking some of Links thunder and payoff money.

But Fernandez was intent to dominate everything that happened in NDW from that moment on. Except for one thing.

He couldn't stop Cruise and I from doing what ever we wanted. Come to think about it, he badly wanted Cruise and I to flop. The Cruise World Order was very hot pretty much every time we went out and preformed. Fans began to show up and they were split into two very different groups. First were the savvy fans that really enjoyed our satire of the wrestling business. Those folks got what we were trying to do and had a great time stirring up the others.

The second group were true believers, everything was real to them. They truly hated us. Man, we really got a ton of heat and I ain't lying about that.

One night The Dirty White Boy's wife came up to me, "I just want to warn you, John. A lot of the fans really hate your guts."

I replied, "That's great because I hate them too. After all, that is my job to get heat."

"No, you don't understand. They don't care for my husband. And they really hate Chris Cruise. But they want to see your head on a pole! You need to be very careful out there."

I never forgot that and was cautious coming and going from the armory every night.

Suspended!

New Dimension Wrestling group was really doing a good job drawing fans, attendance was now typically two fifty to three hundred. For a small independent that was pretty good..

We ran shows out of Thomasville, Burlington and in Greensboro at the old ballpark. The ballpark shows were paid for by the Greensboro Bats, a lot of people stayed to watch wrestling after the baseball game.

One day Chris Cruise came up with the idea to have matches every Thursday night in Thomasville. They created handouts announcing this revolution in wrestling. Cruise and Chris Plano thought this was going to be a big hit.

Cruise was going to put up the money to finance these three shows. No one asked me if this was a good idea. I knew this was going to fail but a fool and his money are soon parted so I watched as things began to fall apart.

The idea was to copy Memphis Wrestling's matches every Monday night. Now that I think about it, when was the last time Memphis ever made a buck?

The first night we drew about 75 people. It was a tough crowd too. I really don't think that any of our regulars showed and a cold crowd isn't a good thing. Not good for the Cruise World Order that much is for sure. No one got what we were doing, we were dead on arrival. I did everything I could think of to insult these people and they just sat on their hands all night.

It is amazing how big the ring gets when you have no heat.

We were quick to beat it back to the dressing room where Manny Fernandez was in Plano's ear cutting us to pieces. I swear, he was happy when we finally failed and put us down mercilessly. That is something I will never forget. He was drawing no one and was quick to kill us at his first chance.

I was stunned, after all weren't we all on the same team?

Anyway, this experiment lasted three shows and I think Thursday went on twice until we went back to Saturday night. Chris Cruise did break even and I was really happy he didn't loose a lot of cash. Didn't make any but that's show biz.

Well, a month later, one Saturday night, things got crazy.

As the show started I noticed a local fan named Wahoo on the front row. This guy I knew from the independent shows in Salisbury. He was a total nut job that yelled all night at the Heels saying witty things like, "Do me like that!" and, "Wah-Whooooooooo!"

Needless to say, he was no Rhodes Scholar. I wasn't going to put up with that shit all night so I decided to strike first. As Cruise and I walked to the ring I threw a cold glass of water on him and yelled, "Shut up, Wahoo!" That stunned the guy and we didn't hear a word out of him for the rest of the night.

In the ring, for some reason, Chris Cruise decided to fan the heat by yelling at Chris Plano's girlfriend. It was very funny at the time but Plano didn't smarten this chick up, she thought we were messing with her on a personal level. Cruise is the kind of guy that, when he has somebody really pissed off, that means he is just warming up, he never takes any prisoners. This girl, I am not going to use her name, was taking admissions at the front door. Cruise just went off on her. His first line was, "HEY! Where is Plano's bitch?"

Now is that reason to get angry? Hell yes if you take into consideration that sitting right next to the girl was her mother!

Man, the shit hit the fan like I have rarely ever seen. But I had to back up Cruise right? So I said something about she looked like someone on Jerry Springer. This girl and her mother went off big time and ran to the ring yelling at the top of her lungs that we suck. It was a gold mine.

The crowd went crazy yelling with her "to kick our asses." It was crazy heat, I wish you had been there. When we went back to the dressing room this chick was screaming at Plano, "Chris, I don't care how good these guys are! I don't care how much heat they can get! You have to choose! It is either them or me!" That's a quote.

Cruise snapped, "Jesus woman! Can't you understand that it is all work! You stupid BITCH!" Have I ever mentioned that at one time Chris Cruise once studied to be a priest? I guess you can tell how this turned out.

We were suspended on the spot. And that lasted for seven months.

Remember this, wrestling fan—never have a man choose between you and his lay.

We Have Met the Enemy and He is Us!
(A quote from the great Walt Kelly)

Being away from the squared circle was not as painful as I expected. Life went on. A little less exciting but I owned and managed a comic book store so I had plenty to keep me busy. But the pull to get back in the ring and cause trouble was a strong one.

Both Chris Cruise and I stayed away from New Dimension Wrestling for seven months, I never even went to an armory show once. Believe me, I wanted to. With all the heat we had I thought it would be rude for us to just show up and sit in the audience. It seemed too markish to even attempt to take away from what was happening in the ring. I really do have that kind of respect for the athletes that work so hard to take any of their heat.

Even a little would just be wrong. So I stayed home.

We did return after the seven months and, man, what a mess we came back to. Crowds had shrunk to about seventy-seven people total. It was a real shock because the last time we worked there was about three hundred and fifty.

New Dimension was nearly dead and I felt really badly about it. Cruise did as well, we both knew it would be pretty tough to get this group re-energized again. Cruise and I were supposed to do a run in and be a surprise at the end of the show. We were really fired up and arrived at the Thomasville armory two hours early so no one would see us and spoil the big return.

Now what would you do to set up the return of The Cruise World Order? I suggested we do a run in to attack Rick Link and put him in the hospital, setting up another long, somewhat profitable run.

Or maybe walk out at the end of a match and beat the shit out a jobber so everyone would know we were the bad guys.

Or even better, hire a few wrestlers to run in and attack Link, beating him senseless. And then have us walk out seeking our revenge!

Or bring in a big name, Stan Hansen or Abdullah the Butcher, and kick the shit out of the guy. Hell Yeah! That always works!

We would lose money but it would be worth it in the long run. I could see it now, New Dimension Wrestling! Anything could happen!

Well, that didn't happen. The ring came apart after the second match so we were sent out to just walk around and fill the time so they could fix the ring.

When we did walk out there was a pop from the crowd of faithful that still attended the matches. But the Cruiser and I were pretty hot over this turn of events, we went after Chris Plano with both barrels. Plano was in the ring, turned, then began to question why we were at the show.

Funny, I always thought that anything you said in the ring was forgiven if it got heat. But that sometimes is not the truth.

I looked at Plano and said, "Hey Plano! What happened? The last time we were here we wrestled in front of three hundred and fifty people. We leave for seven months and now you are packing in about seventy-seven! You sure know how to run a promotion in to the ground!"

The truth hurts a little too much for Plano and he said something to me after the show. He wasn't happy about being reminded that his NDW was falling apart. It really is amazing that the guy who owns the promotion didn't even get the idea that we had to establish ourselves as the bad guys quickly.

If you think about it, if we did go over huge he makes more money.

Anyway, we stood on the ringside floor filling time as they fixed the damn ring. Come to think about it, that ring was never the same once the Sergeant was fired. That guy could work wonders with that death trap. And the ring apron was flat out nasty with old bloodstains all over it. The thing was never cleaned once in the two years I was on it. We were all very lucky to escape with out catching a serious staph infection.

We both felt like idiots working the crowd but we did it anyway then retreated back to the dressing room to just sit there.

But a great thing happened that night, a young wrestler came up to me and asked if he could be a part of our action. The wrestler was named Steele and he looked just like a teenage Opie Taylor. The whole thing was really funny. Steve 'Steele' Greene asked me to beat his ass at the next show.

And I knew exactly what to do. It would be perfect.

Would this scare a kid or what?

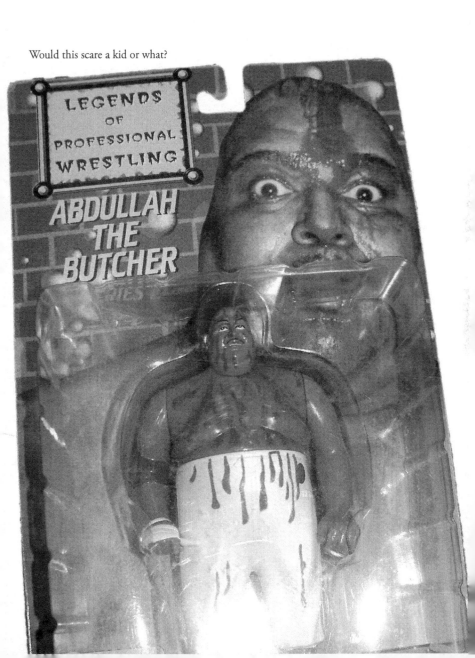

Back in the Groove

Now with "Steele" on board willing to do whatever we told him things seemed to make much more sense. It was a perfect opportunity to get everyone over with a cold crowd.

And this is what we did.

The first or second match Steele would wrestle a bigger wrestler and sell everything for him. Our goal was to establish he had guts and was a solid worker. After about five to six minutes of getting beaten the crowd began to feel sorry for him and was cheering for him. The match really looked like a slaughter but at the very end Steele would duck a clothesline and hit the Stone Cold Stunner for the shocking win out of nowhere.

This always worked and Steele got a big pop from the crowd.

Then the ring announcer would interview Steele, who really did look like Opie Taylor, telling the crowd this match was his very first win in wrestling. He then would say that he had been working very hard in the gym and was hoping one day to gain the fans respect.

Just as this underdog babyface was winning the crowd over, Cruise and I would hit the ring asking this chump if he realized this time was reserved for our interview, not his. And why was he still in our ring?

Just as Steele would begin to explain I would whack him from behind with a cooking pan to the back of his head. Give Steele credit, he sold it like it was a gunshot blast, then Chris Cruise would continue to beat him down even as he was being carried from the ring.

That pan shot was a lucky thing for us. Cruise came up with this foreign object that, when you hit someone with it, it made a huge ringing noise. It really did sound like we KO'd the guy but he was fine.

Steele seemed to enjoy it.

This whole deal worked wonders on the crowd, everybody knew we were the bad guys after that.

I always thought it important to establish early on who the wrestlers to boo for were and it was a very easy thing to set up. Every dumb ass that went to a NDW show knew within five minutes what was going on.

Simple always works.

After our interview informing everyone who we were going to fight in the main event we barreled back to the dressing room.

Once Cruise and I got to the back we sat down with Steele to make sure he was cool with everything we did to him. I will never forget that moment. Steele looked up and thanked me for beating his ass. As it turned out he was considering giving this whole wrestling thing up because the fans had always told him he sucked. That night was the first time he every got cheered.

He then asked if next time he could juice? Steele was our boy from then on.

Cruise Rules

Every once in awhile wrestling could get totally out of hand and become kind of scary for people like myself.

I like wrestling when everything goes smooth just the way it suppose to. Or at least talked about. Or agreed upon by every one involved.

One night Cruise and I attacked Steele after his match., this was something we always did. For some reason, the guy who wrestled Steele became unhinged and decided he wanted to kick our ass.

Funny thing about wrestling, you can talk with a guy, book his match and things are understood but still wrestlers can get over-excited and go nuts. I remember yelling at this masked guy to get out of the ring except he got even more upset that we were beating up his friend.

Look Dude, we are trying to get some heat!

I swear I totally broke character trying to wake this guy up to the fact he was ruining the show. Finally he had to be told by Steele that everything was fine and to please leave the ring. That kind of thing happened every few shows.

Wrestlers get that I am going to be a star shit and steal more ring time for themselves than they were suppose to get. A great wrestling match relies on timing and rhythm. I have rarely been in the middle of one that was prefect and accomplished exactly what we wanted. But I did try to make sense out of everything.

In Thomasville, Cruise and I got evolved in a match-up that was totally out of control. For a short period of time, Chris Cruise and I managed to turn Manny Fernandez on Rick Link. Not a bad idea but all we were doing was repackaging a routine that everyone there had seen a dozen times before.

Trust me, you can only polish a turd so many times.

Anyway, the next match we wanted Manny to destroy Link but he had second thoughts and booked the match where he turns on us.

Manny refused to kill Link and he did the turn. Just as it looked like Manny was going to squash Cruise, I ran up to the ring to make the save. (For you folks lost, that was my job to take the bump for Chris Cruise so he could escape. It was the old carrot on a stick idea. Why I always took the beating I have no idea. I graduated from college, made the Dean's List.)

Going for the save Manny booted me in the stomach. To be totally honest, he took care of me and didn't kick very hard. I sold it like crazy you can bet on that. Just as it looked like the end of the Cruise World Order five new wrestlers ran out and attacked Manny. It was one of those really sad ill-timed attacks too.

Manny was up for a pile driver when the new guys stopped in the middle of the move and waited for Link to run in and make the save. Remember, Link weighs about four hundred and fifty pounds. He ain't going anywhere quick.

It was a real botched spot and I was yelling for them to pile drive Manny but they just stood there looking very stupid. You really had to be there to see Manny hanging upside down in the air. Finally Link made the save and the rematch was set for next month.

Well, the next show was a huge tag match with Link and Manny versus those five or six new wrestlers managed by Cruise and Hitchcock. Cruise told everyone that this match was under the "Cruise Rules". The rules were there are no rules.

Anything goes and the match can only stop by pin fall. The really funny part was that the referee totally believed it. So this mess just went on forever and ever.

One other thing to mention, those five or six wrestlers in the ring that we were managing, well, most of them didn't know how to wrestle. They were never trained, couldn't take a bump, and couldn't work a match if their sorry lives depended on it. We had to manage this turkey shoot.

I swear, it was such a damn mess, I tried to just walk away from the ring but Cruise wouldn't let me.

Chris Cruise, what a pro. (Now that is the funniest thing I have ever written!)

The only reason I bring this night up is that one of these wrestlers grabbed the ring bell and ran around the ring with it. In mid-step the guy tripped and fell face first right on the bell. And the bell rang when he fell on it. I was laughing like crazy and will never forget that moment.

Manny and Link were really pissed about this fiasco and threatened those clowns with a beating when they got to the dressing room. One of the wrestlers named Harold was yelling back that he was hardcore! It was amazing to watch this guy rip his own shirt yelling that he was a real tough guy.

So if you go to a small independent wrestling match you never know just what you will see. Believe me, I was booking the damn show and I never knew half the time.

How to properly use a pan

Wrestling is an odd business. Once you get on a show everyone wants to have a small part of the action. Or maybe it was a way to grab a little glory. Everybody wants in on the act, you have to say "no" more than "yes," that much is for sure.

The two times I said "yes" worked out better than I could have ever dreamed. Both times it was the perfect way to get us heat and get us over as the toughest guys on the planet. Or the biggest jerks in the room.

I must, before, I forget add the first guy that sold the pan shot was Big Eddie Beason. Hitting Eddie and having him sell it got us over more than anything we could have thought of.

One time a friend of mine named Tree (Not his name but I figure this is a good time to protect the innocent and his friends will know exactly whom I am talking about.), He started going to all the New Dimension shows sitting on the Front Row raising hell every night.

My kind of guy. And every show he would yell for me to give him a pan shot. So one day, I figured why not?

I talked it out with Cruise, Tree was set to get the pan shot in our next show at the Burlington Armory.

Tree had a friend with him who was not hip to the idea and, lets face it, he was a mark. I guess we should have smartened the guy up but I felt that was Tree's job not mine.

When the moment came Cruise and I walked to the ring while Tree is screaming at us like a crazed man. You couldn't possibly miss this guy on the front row, I pointed Tree out so Cruise knew who to go after. After about three minutes, of this Cruise snapped, leaped out of the ring and started to hammer the guy. One thing I should mention, Chris Cruise is a very agile guy. I think he was a squirrel in his past life because he was fast as hell.

Tree was perfect in his role, he didn't back down an inch and yelled right back at Cruise. Then I stepped up and got between them. I shouted to

Cruise that this was an old friend of mine and I knew how to handle him.

Cruise looked at me and told me to take care of this guy. As Cruise turned to the ring, I did a pivot move and turned blindly and nailed Tree square on the head. That pan shot sounded like a bomb going off, Tree sold it like a champ, falling dead to the ground. I swear, Tree acted like he was unconscious, selling the dreaded pan shot as well as anyone could.

The crowd went berserk.

But the guy that really made a scene was Tree's buddy. I never knew his name but he just about jumped the rail to go after both of us for killing his friend. He wasn't a very tall guy but he sure was hot.

I just looked him right in the eyes and said, "I just knocked out the toughest guy in Burlington with one shot! And if you want some you little pussy, come get some!"

Truly, one of my proudest moments.

I think the security stepped up to grab his crazy guy and stopping him from hitting the ring. The funny part was we never thought to smarten up the security! Tree sold that knock out shot so well security got a little frightened and propped Tree up in a chair.

Man, the look on the security guard's face was priceless.

After writing this story I began to think the pan shot to a friend wasn't the best idea we ever had. Thank God every guy we hit with the dreaded pan always sold it. Imagine what would happen if someone didn't... it would have killed the gimmick.

I think we would have moved over to a metal canteen if the pan was exposed for what it was.

The next New Dimension Wrestling show was going to be in my hometown, Greensboro, North Carolina, with the usual gang of wrestlers and a main event from days past, Jimmy "The Boogie Woogie Man" Valiant. Valiant was a big deal in New York, Memphis and probably had his biggest run in the Mid-Atlantic territory during the middle 1980s.

Back then I used to boo the poor sap and never thought of Boogie as a great wrestler. But he was a good draw and a solid, very funny interview. The fans in the Mid-Atlantic loved the guy for years but now he was cashing in on his past, working the small time independents and running his wrestling school.

So what can you do with this guy and be original? And understand Boogie is not going to do a moonsault on Chris Cruise for a finish.

Boogie always told everyone in earshot, and I quote, "Boogie don't take no bumps, brother." So I decided to have some fun with this and booked a match that, with a little luck, everyone would enjoy. I went up to Valiant and told him what we wanted to do, he loved it except for the finish. We had asked him to do an elbow smash on Cruise for the finish but he told us he'd do a sleeper finish instead.

That was cool as far as I was concerned and Boogie seemed very happy with the set-up I suggested. But as I laid out the match to Valiant, Chris

Cruise walked away laughing. A little later I asked Cruise what was the deal? Cruise looked at me and said, "John you just don't get it. I grew up in Maine and watched the Valiant Brothers on TV when I was a kid. This guy is like a childhood idol to me and here you are standing there telling him what to do in a match! It is just too strange for me to watch. But you have balls, that much is for sure."

I never even thought about it that way, all I was after was to have a new interesting match. Hell, I knew we were not going over. No big deal but it would be a lot of fun.

Well, the show started and about 250 folks showed up including my sister and her two children, John Thomas and Amy Ann. They were not wrestling fans and were bored to death most of the night.

The show started as usual with Steele selling his ass off for the whole match then, out of nowhere, winning with the stone cold stunner. We had a guest ring announcer, a DJ from 102 JAMS who really didn't know what he was getting himself in for as Cruise and I stormed into the ring. I just went off on the guy, telling him I listened to ROCK92 and he needed to get out of our ring. I think he wanted to take a swing at me but he did get out of the ring.

Steele, and I cannot overstate this enough, was tremendous in putting us both over. Cruise was yelling at him while I panned him from behind, like a good heel should. The crowd really ate this up, about half just fell over laughing. Yeah, they were friends of mine in shock at the transformation from mild mannered comic book store owner to a heelish asshole. My family was in shock, too.

We began to talk a lot of trash about Valiant. Suddenly, an old Front Row friend Fritz Grondy began to yell at us to shut up and sit down, that we sucked. Not a topic that we wanted to discuss. Cruise got pissed, jumped out of the ring and just hammered the guy (thankfully with little profanity). Anyway, I got between them and told Cruise this was an old friend and I would set things right. As Cruise returned to the ring I panned Fritz with a beautiful, out of nowhere shot. It was perfect.

I had to hand it to Fritz, he sold that pan shot for about 45 minutes while the crowd lost it. Security dragged him to the front communality center where he continued selling. He scared a few of the young kids in attendance but it put us over as the bad guys and that was what we wanted.

Then Cruise and I told everyone that the old guy out front selling Boogie Woogie tapes and merchandise was, in reality, some old homeless person screwing them out of their hard earned coin. This was a shoot comment, for years the real Valiant relentlessly sold tapes at every Wal-Mart in North Carolina he could get a break from. It became an expected part of every independent show, he was chasing every buck he could.

Well, we beat it back to the dressing room and waited for the main event. Those times in the back waiting could really suck because you just sat there as the rest of the show marches on. If you were lucky we would have some old pro to tell road stories but sometimes it was three long hours of waiting.

First Cruise came out to the ring alone to tell the fans that he wanted to wrestle Valiant right now. Some sort of music started to play, not Valiant's regular theme I asked the dumbass sound guy to play. For my entrance I stepped out with a mop on my head dancing around like The Boogie Woogie Man. The audience loved the comedy and we roasted Valiant but good.

Cruise was acting as a ring announcer so we really went for broke. "The Pussy Wussy Man is here!" I said, "Tony Schvantoe! It is great to be back in North Kac-a- lack-eee!"

Cruise fired back, "I am not Tony, and I am not that fat. You dumb ass!"

I told him it was great to be back in the Greensboro Coliseum. Cruise, as dry as possible, said I was an idiot, this wasn't the Coliseum but some crappy armory. I then said, "The Boogie Man feels mighty low."

Every minute or so, I would jump around the ring kicking the ropes and saying "Mercy" over and over for the full Valiant impression. Everybody but my family seemed to enjoy this farce.

I warned Cruise I'd teach him, "The Rufus R Jones three-step bump". The three-step bump is a staple for older wrestlers to fall down during a match and not get hurt. Cruise would hit me and I would grab the top rope. Cruise would then hit me again, and I would go to one knee. Then the third step, I would roll over to the mat.

What a warrior.

All this time the real Valiant was creeping to the ring to beat us up. The crowd got behind all this nonsense, which we were very grateful for. Valiant grabbed me on the floor and gave me his signature kiss. As I backed up turning around he hit me and I fell to the tile floor. It's times like this I wished I had some sort of training, I was seeing stars from the fall. Valiant then hit the ring and beat up Cruise and finished him with the sleeper. As Cruise lay passed out, Valiant then pulled Cruises pants off to reveal that he was wearing a funny pair of colored shorts. We then ran back to the dressing room. My leader was supposed to be wearing women's underwear but he chickened out. What a pussy!

Another day, another twenty bucks.

Big Jay

My wonderful wrestling career was winding down and I didn't even know it. The large crowds were beginning to return after Cruise and I were suspended so I was very optimistic about our future in a small time wrestling company.

Silly me. Everyone wants to get in the act.

There was a friend of mine who was really fired up to get into the ring. His name was Big Jay and he's one huge, strong, nice guy. Jay played football in South Carolina for a few years and was an obsessed wrestling fan.

In the world of independents, this would qualify you for a training program. Jay wanted to skip that step just like Cruise and I had done. I was booking all of our matches so it was time for Big Jay to hit the ring. And another thing, we had started every show trashing Steele for months. It really was time to change up that program.

Now understand, I was not expecting Jay to moonsault the first match out. It would be really funny but I didn't want him falling on me so we decided to keep his participation very basic.

I had a solid idea how to pull this off, first I went to the hardware store to buy a large metal trash can. That was easy enough to work with, it did hurt a little. I was spending more than I was going to make at the show but that's small time wrestling.

Night of the big show about 180 people turned out at Thomasville and ready for action. Sadly what they got from the Cruise World Order was not really wrestling.

This is what happened.

Steele once again won his match after taking a beating from his opponent. Cruise and I hit the ring and, once again, we panned him with a beautiful headshot. For some reason, we dallied in the ring to yell at all the fans ringside. Steele got up and picked up the deadly pan that was lying in the ring. That was pretty stupid of me, Steele tapped me on the shoulder and panned me, knocking me to the ring floor. Needless to say, the crowd was enthusiastically cheering him on, hoping Cruise would finally gets his. Then, out of nowhere, Big Jay hit the ring to save the Cruise World Order.

I was relived but there was a major surprise when Jay slid into the ring with a face-first slide. That normally wouldn't be a problem except he was wearing sweat pants. When he hit the ring, his pants didn't go with him! There was Big Jay standing in the ring half naked. Proving just how big he really was!

The crowd went crazy laughing and yelling at the NDW version of the Shock Master. That didn't slow Big Jay down one bit; he grabbed the pan from a stunned Steele and smacked him with it. Then he jerked Steele up for a press slam and followed up with a big elbow smash.

Poor Steele didn't know what hit him. And I couldn't believe Jay was breaking the script and punishing the guy. Jay finally helped me up and told Cruise he wanted us to train him to be a wrestler. What a guy!

Steele staggered to his feet and grabbed the house microphone to cut this promo on us. "Hey, you slack jawed motherfucker! Nobody can jump me like that and get away with it! I want a match with you here tonight!"

Cruise, Dirty White boy, Big Jay and yours truly accepted that challenge. Cruise looked at me and told me to train Big Jay for his up coming match. "Teach him everything you know." Considering I knew very little that was an easy request.

In the back room Steele was a little put out by Big Jay's unexpected move, taking liberties during his run in, so I had Jay go over and tell him he was sorry. An apology can go a long way to keep an angle going. The Dirty White Boy wanted to know if it was okay now for us to say motherfucker over the ring microphone. Steele turned white with embarrassment. He said he never remembered saying that. Everyone in the back room laughed that one off for hours.

A few matches later, Big Jay squared off against the Opie Taylor of NDW. Cruise once again asked me if I had trained Big Jay. Of course. The match started with Jay and Steele locking up collar and elbow. (I always wanted to write that.) Jay pushed Steele into the ring corner to hit him with a few shoulder blocks. Jay then put a headlock on Steele, walked to the middle of the ring and sat down.

Everyone in the Cruise World Order celebrated! A minute went by with Jay still sitting in the ring with a headlock on Steele.

Then three minutes went by and Jay still sat there with the same headlock.

I asked Jay if he was under control and he said, "I got him. I can beat him any time!"

At the four-minute mark the crowd got kind of hostel yelling for Jay to do something. Then Cruise was yelling at me to get Jay to do something. I told him that was all I knew about wrestling so that was all he was going to do.

At five minutes White Boy started screaming at me to fix this. Of course Cruise was showing his support by screaming at me calling me an idiot, demanding me to do something, anything because this match sucked.

Funny, Cruise seemed to enjoy yelling at me, and I booked this angle. Note to John, book and angle where I yell at Cruise a lot calling him an asshole.

Slowly I walked to the back room and returned with a shiny new garbage can. The White Boy grabbed the can and got in the ring. He then told Big Jay to stand up; he was going to teach him how to wrestle. Thinking back I think he called Big Jay pork chop or something like that.

Steele slowly stood up selling the punishing headlock just as White Boy hit him once with the metal trash can. White Boy was supposed to hit him three or four times but one was more than enough. That can shot was the loudest thing I have ever heard at a wrestling match, it folded around Steele's head and the crowd went crazy. Big Jay and the Dirty White Boy left the ring and Cruise and I celebrated like six year olds at Christmas. As we walked to the back room, the referee announced that the winner of the match was Steele due to outside interference. We all protested this and demanded a rematch at the next show.

But there was never going to be a next NDW show for the Cruise World Order. NDW was only going to do paid baseball shows from then on and Cruise was moving up to DC to except a new job.

After everyone returned to the back room I went over to check on Steele. He was fine. The can shot didn't hurt him too much. That really shocked me because, trust me, everybody there that night will never forget that move. Steele did have one major complaint. He wanted me to ask Big Jay to please start using some deodorant in the future. Turns out poor Steele was being gassed during the whole angle.

There was never a more dedicated wrestler than Steve "Steele" Green, he even asked me if he could be the juice in the next match.

What a guy!

About 6 years later Big Jay passed away from a stroke. Jay was tremendous, you had to love him. I miss him a lot.

My lunch with Rip

The Legends reunion shows in Charlotte are an amazing experience for wrestling fans. Back in the sixties and seventies there were rumors that wrestlers would stop at certain curb markets on their way back to Charlotte where you could actually meet them in person. When I would

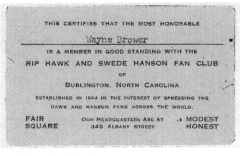

pass one of these stores I would think, Black Bart stopped here once. Or Terry Funk once bought a handful of snickers there. The other thing was if you were a Greensboro fan you saw the greatest matches of all time and saw the greatest wrestlers too. Biggest building could sell the most tickets so Greensboro fans had it made but we never met the wrestlers. Ever. They would pile into their cars and head back to Charlotte and wouldn't party here.

These reunions changed that. If you made any effort you could meet just about every wrestler you ever wanted to. Matter of fact, if you purchased a book they were selling you could ask a few questions and believe it or not get real answers with no bullshit.

I was up in my room taking a break when I got a phone call from my friend Wayne Brower. He told me to get my ass down to the lobby, we could have lunch with Rip Hawk. Shit.

I got down there as fast as I could. Rip Hawk was one of a few legends from my childhood that I really wanted to meet. It was just dumb luck I got this chance. At first it was odd but Rip just was flat out friendly. He looked at the waitress at the bar and told her he could not believe we even knew who he was. Hard to imagine that anyone could be that humble but he was.

I peppered him with questions and he was honest and open about everything. Rip told us John Ringley was a smart idea guy who drew up the Mid-Atlantic logo seen on TV. Ringley was fired because he got caught cheating on the Crockett daughter. Rip said it was a big loss because he was so savvy about business, a very smart guy.

Something I had to ask about was the story of Brute Bernard scaring my brother Sparky back in the dressing room, drooling on himself. Was that a work?

Rip said, No, Brute was flat out crazy as hell. That was just the way he was. Rip told a story about riding with Brute and stopping off at his favorite diner for lunch. He made a point of telling Brute that these were good people to deal with, rare in that they never bothered anyone while they were eating. Well, as they began lunch Brute started slipping into character, yelling at the waitress, making a spectacle of himself. It was a goddamn mess and Rip quickly got up and left the restaurant. He was really pissed off at Brute. As they drove down the highway, Rip went off on him, threatening to kick the shit out of him. Rip pulled over at a flower stand and ordered Brute to get out and buy that waitress some flowers and they would go back and he would apologize. If he didn't Rip would stomp his ass. Brute did purchase some roses and went back to the dinner. Brute walked in and asked for the frightened waitress. As she approached the front he snapped and began smashing the flowers on the cash register yelling in that Bernard way. Obviously the whole restaurant was rattled and frightened.

Rip said he watched the whole thing in shock. When Brute returned to the car, Rip just went off on the guy and told him to find another ride to the shows because that was it as far as their friendship went.

The toughest was to come.

Rip asked me if I knew what happened to his partner Swede Hansen. This was not something I wanted to cover but he insisted. The Big Swede had gotten engaged to a fan and was living with her in a nice trailer. One day she came home to find Hansen in a violent rage. He was wrecking the interior of the trailer. Hansen was a very strong guy, something had set him off and he was not consolable and broke everything in sight. The woman that loved and cared for him had no choice but call the police and it took about six cops to subdue Hansen. He was taken to a hospital for psychiatric care. Sadly, Hansen never left the hospital and died there locked up in a padded cell. I did make sure to add, he should ask around because this is what I heard and I could be wrong. Wrestling rumors are rampant so I was trying to soften the blow. Rip said Swede was like a brother to him and he would miss him the rest of his life.

Later Rip and Wayne stayed and drank the bar closed. Wayne bragged that Rip and Wayne were now the Mid-Atlantic drinking champions. Rip laughed and said, "Yeah, those young guys never could learn to drink."

Last Words

There are lots of other stories about wrestling that I could tell but it is time to put this book to bed. But here a few more I need to mention.

Cruise and I actually did get to manage the Iron Sheik in Lexington, NC. It was a lot of fun, The Sheik was a very nice open guy to talk with. Of course, during his match with Rick Link he turned on me and put me in his Camel Clutch for the finish. Only one problem, we both lost our balance and he fell over beside me. I was mortified but then again I broke the WWE Hall of Famer's hold which makes me the only man ever to break the feared Camel Clutch. All my friends hear that story endlessly.

One night in Greensboro Simp and I talked this crazy fan into jumping the rail to attack Nikita Koloff. I got an elbow from Simp and he said, "I got a live one." This person was wired and hated the Russians. He really did grab Nikita by the leg and hold on for dear life waiting for us to jump in and assist. We failed to mention that we weren't helping; he spent the night in jail.

One friend of my brother Bob named Scotty claimed the high honor of being thrown out of the Coliseum for grabbing Buddy Rogers as he walked by. Scotty grabbed Rogers arm and said, "Big Elbows Man, Big Elbs." Walking to the ring with Rogers was Jimmy Snuka and John Studd and they didn't lift a finger during this mess. Scotty got tossed but bought another ticket and sat with us and promptly passed out in a chair for the rest of the night. Another first, two tickets for one show!

Now that I think about it alcohol may have been involved with Scotty's hijinks.

Funny the way life works. After a while of the Front Row being seen on television week after week folks began to notice. Matter of fact, my nephews started calling wrestling the 'Uncle John Show' because I was always there. One time we were on Crockett and WWE for about four weeks straight. Anyway, odd things started happening like people calling me on the phone to ask wrestling questions and I didn't know who the hell they were!

"Hey, ahh, is this the wrestling guy? Aaaahhh, will Magnum ever come back to wrestle?"

This happened all the time at my comic book store. My name and phone number got passed around so nutcases started calling. Then again, the name of my store is Parts Unknown so now those crazy calls make sense.

But the classic story was the time my old pal Ken Crutchfield called and asked me to stop by to talk wrestling with his new in-laws. Crutch was my wing man all during the seventies and we watched every wrestling show for years. So I went over to Crutch's house and a guy was there asking some very basic questions. This went on for about an hour and a half before I decided to go for the door. I was tired and wanted to hit the sack. As I'm leaving Crutch told the guy he could ask one last question because I knew all the answers and this was something he had been really looking forward to. Out of nowhere came the question.

"You know those Ninjas in Texas? Are they really Ninjas?"

Many thanks for buying this book. If you got a laugh out of it then I am very happy. This is memory lane for me. And if I did my job then it brought back memories for you too.

One more thing I would like to add. Try to remember all those amazing, talented wrestlers that brought you so much entertainment. Many now are old and in wheelchairs having paid a tremendous price wrestling for their pay checks. Few retired and got rich. So if you meet an old star or jobber, thank them.

What was I thinking? I wasn't. Worst photo of me ever, wearing a Nikita Koloff gym shirt. Great photo of the Nature Boy...

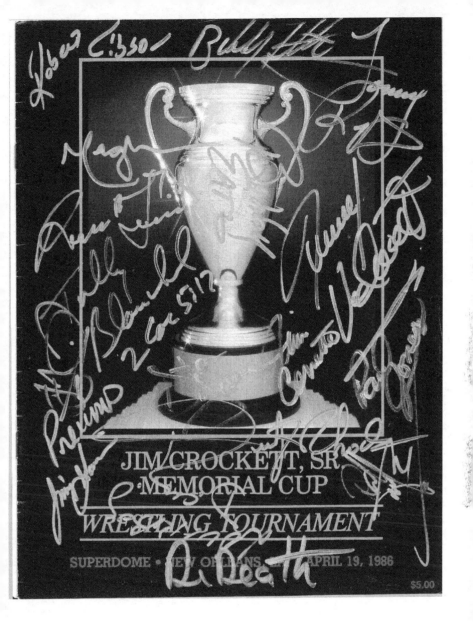

JIM CROCKETT, SR.
MEMORIAL CUP
WRESTLING TOURNAMENT

SUPERDOME • NEW ORLEANS • APRIL 19, 1986

$5.00

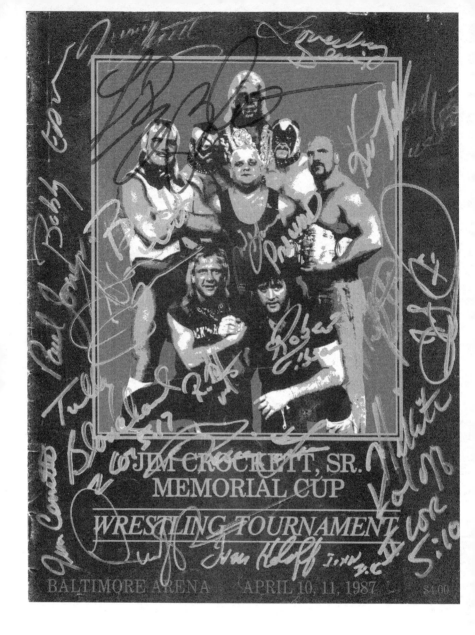

JIM CROCKETT, SR.
MEMORIAL CUP

WRESTLING TOURNAMENT

BALTIMORE ARENA · APRIL 10, 11, 1987 · $4.00

WCW WORLD CHAMPIONSHIP WRESTLING ℠

RICKY MORTON

About the Author

John Hitchcock graduated from Greensboro College with a major in painting in 1978. He is a Greensboro, North Carolina native and life-long Professional Wrestling fan. This is John's second book. The first, *Dear John, The Alex Toth Doodle Book,* was honored with an Eisner Award nomination in 2006. He was featured in the documentary film about the life of artist Alex Toth in 2007.

Hitchcock is an artist, storyteller, sort-of wrestler, and owner of Parts Unknown The Comic Book Store for the last twenty five years. Single (and quit looking for love a long time ago) leaves John plenty of time for his next book, Comic Book People, about the famous artists and writers he has been friends with for the last thirty years and counting.

BITTER OLD FAN.

Made in the USA
San Bernardino, CA
09 May 2015